CW00550822

An Old Coachman's Chatter, With Some Practical Remarks On Driving

Edward Corbett

AN

OLD COACHMAN'S CHATTER

WITH SOME

Practical Remarks on Driving.

BY

A SEMI-PROFESSIONAL,

EDWARD CORBETT,

Colonel late Shropshire Militia.

With Eight full-page Illustrations on Stone, by
JOHN STURGESS.

LONDON:

RICHARD BENTLEY AND SON,
Publishers in Ordinary to Her Majesty the Queen.

1890.

[*The right of Translation and all other rights reserved.*]

Printing Statement:

Due to the very old age and scarcity of this book, many of the pages may be hard to read due to the blurring of the original text, possible missing pages, missing text, dark backgrounds and other issues beyond our control.

Because this is such an important and rare work, we believe it is best to reproduce this book regardless of its original condition.

Thank you for your understanding.

J.Sturgess del.et lith.

M&N Hanhart imp.

WYLE COP. SHREWSBURY. A MINUTE TO 12.

TO

MY QUONDAM PASSENGERS

OF

DAYS GONE BY

𝔍 𝔙enture to 𝔇edicate this 𝔙olume,

THANKING THEM FOR THEIR FORMER SUPPORT

AND

HOPING FOR THEIR KIND PATRONAGE

OF

THIS LITTLE BOOK.

SF 307
C 6

CONTENTS.

M309189

LIST OF ILLUSTRATIONS

ON STONE

By JOHN STURGESS.

ON WOOD.

DIAGRAMS.

b

AN

OLD COACHMAN'S CHATTER,

SOME REMARKS ON DRIVING.

———⊸⊱⊰⊸———

INTRODUCTION.

I THINK it is Dr. Johnson who has somewhere remarked, that "everyone who writes a book should
either help men to enjoy life or to endure it."

Whether these few pages will have the former
effect I know not, but if they only help to dispel
ennui for an hour or two, they will not have been
written quite in vain, and, at any rate, I trust they
will not be found so unendurable as to be unceremoniously thrown out of the railway carriage window,
or behind the fire.

Though several books on the same subject have
been already published, I entertain a hope that this
may not prove "one too many," as the interest taken
in coaching, so far from diminishing, would appear

to be increasing, judging by the number of coaches running out of London and other places, some even facing the inclemency of winter in the love for the road. The number of private drags also never was so large. "Nimrod" put it at twenty to thirty in the early part of the century. It must be nearly four times that now.

I have not the vanity to suppose that I can contribute anything more racy or better told than much that has gone before, but having engaged in coaching as a matter of business, and in partnership with business men, when and where coaches were the only means of public travelling, and having driven professionally for upwards of four years, I have had the opportunity of looking behind the scenes, and have had experiences which cannot have fallen to the lot of most gentlemen coachmen, and certainly will fall to the lot of no others again.

I lay no claim to literary merit, nor will what I offer savour much of the sensational or perhaps of novelty; but this I can say, that it is all drawn from personal knowledge, and that, with the exception of one old friend, who has had great experience on some of the best coaches in England, I am indebted to no one for my facts, which has not been the case in all which has been published, judging from some inaccuracies I have met with. To mention only one, which, if considered for a moment, is so improbable, not to say impossible, that it surely must be a misprint.

In " Highways and Horses " we are told that the fare for one passenger by mails was eight shillings outside and twelve inside for a hundred miles. Why, this is less than Parliamentary trains ! It would have been impossible to have horsed coaches at such prices. The real rate was from fourpence to fivepence per mile inside, and from twopence to threepence outside for that distance. The highest fares were charged by the mails and fast day coaches, the heavy night coaches having to be content with the lower rate.

The reader will observe that I do not confine myself to what were called, *par excellence*, " the palmy days of coaching," but have brought it down to a period twenty years later, when the coaches, though comparatively few, were still running in considerable numbers in out-of-the-way districts, upon the old lines, and by those who had learned their business in those palmy days. The pace was not generally so great, judged by the number of miles to the hour, but, taking into consideration the great inferiority of the roads, there was little or no falling off. Indeed, I doubt whether over some roads, eight miles an hour was not harder to accomplish than ten had been over the better roads. Of course, as in earlier days, the work was unequally done, sometimes good, sometimes bad, and sometimes indifferent.

If these pages should happen to fall into the hands of any of the many thousand passengers I have had the pleasure of driving, and on whom I hope Father Time has laid benevolent hands, perhaps some of them may recognize scenes which they themselves experienced ; and to others memory may bring back the recollection of happy wanderings, thereby causing renewed pleasure. For, as the poet says :

> " When time, which steals our hours away,
>   Shall steal our pleasures too,
>   The memory of the past shall stay,
>   And half our joys renew."

In the remarks on driving, I do not profess to have written a treatise or to have by any means exhausted the subject—that, indeed, were hard to do ; a coachman should be always learning ;—they are the result of having carefully watched old and experienced hands, together with such instructions as they gave me, followed up by long and continuous practice. I know that some, whose opinions are entitled to the greatest respect, hold different views upon some points ; but, at any rate, whether others agree with me or not, they will see, from the examples I have given, that I have practical reasons for all that I advance.

I should like to add that these pages were in MS. previously to the publication of the seventh volume of the Badminton Library, and, indeed, I have not yet had the pleasure of reading it ; therefore, if I have enunciated doctrines the same as are there given, I cannot be accused of plagiarism. I have felt compelled to make this statement on account of the very high authority of the writers in that book, and when we agree, I shall experience the satisfaction of knowing that I travel in good company.

I have been led on by my subject to spread my wings, and fly to southern latitudes ; indeed, I have ventured, like Mr. Cook, to take my readers a personally-conducted tour round the world, I will not say exactly in search of knowledge, though, to most, what I have introduced them to must be an unknown world. So fast, indeed, has the world travelled in the last half century, that it has now become ancient history, indeed, sufficiently out of date to afford interest to an antiquary.

"Seated on the old mail-coach, we needed no evidence out of ourselves to indicate the velocity. The vital experience of the glad animal sensibilities made doubts impossible. We heard our speed, we saw it, we felt it as a thrilling; and this speed was not the product of blind insensate agencies that had no sympathy to give, but was incarnated in the fiery eyeballs of the noblest among brutes, in his dilated nostril, spasmodic muscles, and thunder-beating hoofs."—DE QUINCEY.

AN

OLD COACHMAN'S CHATTER,

WITH SOME REMARKS ON DRIVING.

"GOING DOWN WITH VICTORY.

" *The absolute perfection of all the appointments, their strength, their brilliant cleanliness, their beautiful simplicity, but more than all the royal magnificence of the horses were, what might first have fixed the attention. On any night the spectacle was beautiful. But the night before us is a night of victory, and, behold, to the ordinary display what a heart-shaking addition! Horses, men, carriages, all are dressed in laurels and flowers, oak-leaves and ribbons. The guards as officially His Majesty's servants, and such coachmen as are within the privilege of the Post Office, wear the royal liveries of course, and on this evening exposed to view without upper coats. Such costume, and the laurels in their hats dilate their hearts by giving them a personal connection with the great news. One heart, one pride, one glory, connects every man by the transcendent bond of his national blood. The spectators, numerous beyond precedent, express their sympathy with these fervent feelings by continual hurrahs. Every moment are shouted aloud by the Post-Office servants and summoned to draw up the great ancestral names of cities known to history through a thousand years—Lincoln, Winchester, Portsmouth, Gloucester, Oxford, Bristol, Manchester, York, Newcastle, Edinburgh, Glasgow, Perth, Stirling, Aberdeen—expressing the grandeur of the Empire by the antiquity of its towns, and the grandeur of the mail establishment by the diffusive radiation of its separate missions. Every moment you hear the thunder of lids locked down upon the mail-bags. That sound to each individual mail is the signal for drawing off which is the finest part of the entire spectacle. Then come the horses into play. Horses! can these be horses that bound off with the action and gestures of leopards? What stir! what ferment! what a thundering of wheels! what a trampling of hoofs! what a sounding of trumpets! what farewell cheers! what peals of congratulation, connecting the name of the particular mail, ' Liverpool for ever,' with the name of the particular Victory, ' Salamanca for ever.' The consciousness that all night long, and all the next day, perhaps even longer, many of these mails like fire racing along a train of gunpowder, will be kindling at every instant new successions of burning joy, has an obscure effect of multiplying the victory itself"*—THOMAS DE QUINCEY, *The English Mail-Coach.*

CHAPTER I.

THE ROYAL MAILS.

I is not within the scope of a book on coaching to go behind the time when mail bags were conveyed on wheels, and the coaches became public conveyances, carrying passengers as well as mail bags.

The first mail coach was put on the road between Bristol and London in the year 1784, and it is worthy of remark that it was originated by a man who had previously had no practical knowledge of either post office or road work. In this respect, curiously enough, the same remark applies to what became so very large a business in the Sister Isle, as to be quite a national institution. In the former case Mr. Palmer, to whose energy and perseverance the mail coach owed its existence, was by profession a theatrical manager, whilst the inaugurator of the Irish car business, which grew to such large dimensions as to employ more than a thousand horses, was a pedlar, neither of which businesses would appear to lead to horse and road work.

Bianconi's cars involuntary bring to my mind a

recipe given me many years ago by one of his foremen
for preventing crib-biting in horses.   It would hardly
pass muster with the Society for the Prevention of
Cruelty to Animals, but he declared it was always
effective if applied in the first instance. It was to nip off
a very small piece from the tip of the horse's tongue.
I never tried it, but can quite understand why it was a
cure, as horses almost invariably commence the vice
by licking the manger, and this process rendered the
tongue so tender as to put a summary end to this
preliminary proceeding.

But this by the way. Before, however, carrying the
history of the mails further, I am tempted to introduce
the reader to an account of a highway robbery of
mail bags, which occurred in Yorkshire in the year
1798, and which shows that the change in the way of
conveying the mails was not commenced before it
was wanted.

The following letter from the Post-office in York,
gives a full and graphic account of the circumstance.

"POST-OFFICE, YORK,

"*February 22nd*, 1798.

"SIR,—I am sorry to acquaint you that the post-
boy coming from Selby to this city, was robbed of his
mail, between six and seven o'clock this evening.
About three miles this side Selby, he was accosted by
a man on foot with a gun in his hand, who asked him

if he was the post-boy, and at the same time seizing hold of the bridle. Without waiting for any answer, he told the boy he must immediately unstrap the mail and give it to him, pointing the muzzle of the gun at him whilst he did it. When he had given up the mail, the boy begged he would not hurt him, to which the man replied, ' He need not be afraid,' and at the same time pulled the bridle from the horse's head. The horse immediately galloped off with the boy who had never dismounted. He was a stout man dressed in a drab jacket and had the appearance of a heckler. The boy was too much frightened to make any other remark upon his person, and says he was totally unknown to him.

"The mail contained bags for Howden and London, Howden and York, and Selby and York. I have informed the surveyors of the robbery, and have forwarded handbills this night to be distributed in the country, and will take care to insert it in the first paper published here. Waiting your further instructions, I remain with respect, Sir,

"Your Obliged and Obedient Humble Servant,

"THOS. OLDFIELD."

Although two hundred pounds' reward was offered nothing more was ever found out about this transaction for about eighty years, when the missing bag was discovered in a very unexpected manner, which is so

well described in a notice contained in the *Daily
Telegraph* newspaper of August 24th, 1876, that I
cannot do better than give their account. After
describing the nature of the robbery it goes on
to say, " So the matter rested for nearly eighty years,
and it would probably have been altogether forgotten
but for a strange discovery which was made a few
days ago. As an old wayside public-house, standing
by the side of the high road near Selby, in a district
known as Churchhill, was being pulled down, the
workmen found in the roof a worn and rotten coat, a
southwester hat, and a mail bag marked Selby. This
led to further search, and we are told that in digging
fresh foundations on the site of the old hostel, a large
number of skeletons were found, buried at a small
distance beneath the surface. There can be no doubt
that in what were affectionately known as 'good old
times,' strange scenes occurred at road-side inns,
especially on the great roads running north and west
from London. The highwaymen of those days were a
sort of local Robin Hood, and were only too often on
best of terms with the innkeepers. Nothing, indeed,
is more likely than for the relic of the highwayman's
plunder to be brought to light from out of the
mouldering thatch of an old wayside inn. The
unearthing of the skeletons is a more serious matter,
and looks as if the Selby hostel had, as many old
houses have, a dark history of its own."

The existence of the skeletons was, however, accounted for by archæologists in a more natural, if less sensational manner. They arrived at the conclusion that the spot had been the site of a very old Christian burial ground, whence called Churchhill ; and this opinion would appear to be borne out by the fact of the skeletons having been encased in a very primitive sort of coffin, consisting of nothing more than the trunk of a tree, which had been sawn asunder and hollowed out to receive the body, the two halves being afterwards closed together again. If they had been the victims of foul play, they would probably have been buried without any coffins at all.

The old mail bag, after some dispute about ownership, came into the possession of the Post-Office, and is to be seen in the library of that establishment at the present time.

Like all other new inventions, the change in the manner of conveying the mails was not without its adversaries, and among the different objections raised one was that it would lead to bloodshed. These objectors, who were, I suppose, the humanitarians of the day, grounded their argument on the fact that the post-boys were so helplessly in the power of the highwaymen, that they made no attempt to defend the property in their charge, but only thought of saving their own lives and limbs ; and it is clearly shown by the case adduced that this is what did

happen upon such meetings, and small blame to the
boys either.   But they went on to prophesy, which is
not a safe thing to do.   They said that when the bags
were in the charge of two men, coachman and guard,
well armed, they would be obliged to show fight, which
would lead to carnage.   It was rather a Quaker sort
of argument, but, perhaps, it was "Friends" who
employed it.

Possibly the change did not all at once put a stop
to the attentions of the gentlemen of the road, but as
I have not found in the archives at the General Post-
Office—which are very complete—any records of an
attack upon the mail coaches, we may infer that none
of any moment did occur.   At any rate, the scheme
seems to have met with popular approval, judging by
two cuttings I have seen from newspapers of the
period, which I introduce as conveying the public
opinion of the time.

The first is dated January 19th, 1784, and says,
"Within these last few days Ministers have had
several meetings with the Postmaster-General, Secre-
tary, and other officers of the General Post-Office, on
the subject of the regulation of mails, which is to make
a branch of the Budget this year.   It is proposed that
instead of the mail-cart, there shall be established
carriages in the nature of stage coaches, in the boot
of which the mail shall be carried, and in the inside
four passengers.   The advantages proposed from this

regulation are various. The passengers will defray the whole expense of the conveyance. The progress of the post will be considerably quicker, as the coach is to wait but a certain time in every place, and the time to be marked on the messenger's express, that there be no intermediate delay. The parcels which are now transmitted from one place to another by the common stage coaches and diligences, to the injury of the revenue, will by a restriction be confined to the mail coaches, and, indeed, the public will prefer the security of the General Post-Office to that of the private man ; for the same reason of safety, persons will prefer travelling in these carriages, as measures are to be taken to prevent robbery. The plan is expected to produce a great deal of money, as well as to afford facility and security to correspondence. It will give a decisive blow to the common stages, and in so far will hurt the late tax, but that loss will be amply recompensed. The plan is the production of Mr. Palmer, manager of the Bath Theatre, and he has been present at the conference on the subject."

The other cutting is of the same year, and says : " A scheme is on foot, and will be put in execution on Monday se'ennight, to send by a post coach from the Post-office at eight o'clock in the evening, letters for Bath, Bristol, Bradford, Calne, Chippenham, Coln-brook, Devizes, Henley, Hounslow, Maidenhead, Marlborough, Melksham, Nettlebed, Newbury, Ramsbury, Reading, Trowbridge, Wallingford, and Windsor. The coach is also to carry passengers."

As will be seen from these extracts the Post-office must have made a very good bargain, as they only paid one penny a mile to the horse contractors, which must have been considerably less than the cost of the boys, carts, and horses. Who found the coaches is not stated, but, in later years, though contracted for by the Post-office, they were paid for by the coach proprietors. At any rate, the fares paid by the passengers, of whom only four were carried, must have been very high, for the coach had to pay to the exchequer a mileage duty of one penny, thereby taking away all that was given by the Post-office for the conveyance of the letters.

There are no records to show in what order of rotation the different mail coaches came into existence; but I know that the one to Shrewsbury commenced running in 1785, and many others must have been put on the roads about that time, as I find that in 1786, no less than twenty left London every evening, besides seven that were at work in different parts of England. The work, however, appears to have been very imperfectly performed. The coaches must at first have been cumbersome.

In the year 1786, the coach to Norwich, *viâ* Newmarket, weighed 21 cwt. 2 qrs., and one to the same place, *viâ* Colchester, weighed 18 cwt., which, however, must have been well constructed, as those coaches were known to have carried as many as twenty-two passengers. There was also what was called a cara-van, or three-bodied coach, *via* Ipswich, carrying twelve inside, weighing 21 cwt. 3 qrs., and is stated to have followed the horses very well indeed.

In November, 1786, Bezant's patent coach was first submitted to the post-office, and was first used on the coach roads in the spring of 1787. Previously the mail coaches were very heavy and badly con-structed, and made of such inferior materials that accidents were general and of daily occurrence, so much so that the public became afraid to venture their lives in them.

The general establishment of mail coaches took place in the spring of 1788. The terms on which Mr. Bezant, the patentee of the patent coaches supplied then, was that he engaged to provide and keep them in constant and thorough repair at two pence halfpenny the double mile. At first, from want of system, these coaches were often sent on their journeys without being greased, and generally even without being washed and cleaned, with the result that seldom a day passed that a coach wheel did not fire.

As the business became more and more matured, spare coaches were put on the roads, so that each one on arriving in London should have two complete days

2

for repair.   This increased the number of coaches to
nearly double.   As each came into London it was sent
to the factory at Millbank, nearly five miles off, to be
cleaned, greased, and examined, for which the charge of
one shilling was to be paid for each coach, and this price
included the drawing of the coach to Millbank and back.

Before this arrangement was made, it was nothing
unusual for passengers to be kept waiting for a couple
of hours, whilst some repairs were being done, which
were only discovered to be necessary just as the coach
was about to start, and then the work was naturally
done in such a hasty manner that the coach started in
far from good condition.

The coach masters objected to this payment of one
shilling for drawing and cleaning, and stated that if it
was enforced they would require threepence per mile
instead of one penny, which would have made a difference of twenty thousand pounds a year to the post-
office revenue.   In the end an agreement was made
with the patentee, and the post-office paid the bills.

In 1791, Mr. Bezant, who was an engineer from
Henley-on-Thames, died, and the business fell into
the hands of Mr. Vidler, his partner, and in the
following year there were one hundred and twenty
of those coaches in use on the mail roads.   Their
weight was from 16 cwt. to 16 cwt. 2 qrs.

I have not been able to find any time-bills for
this early stage of the work, and do not, therefore,

know at what pace the mail coaches were expected
to travel, but, judging from the rather unique instruc-
tion issued to a guard in the year 1796, great pace
on the road was not desired. Perhaps, however, this
omission is not important, as the time of arrival at
the journey's end must have depended very much
upon how many accidents were experienced on the
road. It reminds me of the coachman on the Dover
road, who, on being asked by a passenger what time
he arrived in London, replied, "That the proper hour
was six o'clock, but that he had been every hour of
the four-and-twenty after it."

INSTRUCTIONS TO A GUARD GIVEN IN 1796.

"You remember you are to go down with the
coach to Weymouth, and come up with the last
Tuesday afternoon. Take care that they do not
drive fast, make long stops or get drunk. I have
told you this all before."

The following letter addressed in the same year to
one of the horse contractors throws some light upon
the way in which the work was done.

"Some time since, hearing that your harness was
in a very unfit state to do duty, I sent you a set, as is
the custom of the office to supply contractors whose
harness and reins are bad, when they do not attend to
the representatives of the office. The harness cost
fourteen guineas, but, as they had been used a few

times with the 'King's Royal,' Weymouth, you will only be charged twelve for them."

Who would have supposed that from so un-promising a beginning there should have developed the most perfect system of road travelling which the world has ever seen ? Verily, it goes to prove the truth of the old adage that " practice makes perfect."

This same year, on 11th May, the Liverpool and Hull mail coach was stopped by a pressgang outside Liverpool. A rather serious affray took place, but no mischief was done. The Mayor of Liverpool was communicated with, and asked to give such instruc-tions to the lieutenant of the gang as would prevent any further molestation. Probably, the pressgang saw some passengers on the mail which they supposed to be seafaring men, but it goes to show that the relative positions and rights of the different branches of His Majesty's service were not well understood. However this might have been, it appears that the guards and coachmen of the mails were capable of exerting their rights of free passage along the road to, at least, their full extent. In July, 1796, three gentlemen were riding on horseback, when the Liver-pool and Manchester mail coach came up behind them. It would appear that they did not attempt to get out of the way, whereupon the coachman is stated to have used his whip to one of them, and the guard pulled another off his horse, and then brought out his

firearm, and threatened to shoot them. According to
the guard's statement the gentleman, without speaking
a word, stopped the horses of the coach by laying
hold of the reins, and nearly overturned it. The
coachman flogged the gentleman and his horse; the
guard got down and begged them to be off, and when
they were going to strike him he threatened to shoot
them, upon which they let them go. After a full
inquiry from passengers, etc., it was found that the
guard's statement was false, and he was instantly
dismissed, as was also the coachman.

From the following instructions given in 1796, to
a contractor, asking how the coachman should act
under certain circumstances, it appears that passengers
were apt to be very inconsiderate and difficult to
manage in those days, as they continued to be later on.

"Stick to your bill, and never mind what passengers say respecting waiting over time. Is it not the
fault of the landlord to keep them so long? Some
day, when you have waited a considerable time, say
five or eight minutes longer than is allowed by the bill,
drive away and leave them behind, only take care that
you have a witness that you called them out two or
three times. Then let them get forward how they can."

This is much more consideration than was
generally shown in later years.

I was once driving a mail when I had a Yankee
gentleman for one of the outside passengers, who was

disposed to give trouble in this way, and after being
nearly left behind once or twice, he told me that I was
bound to give him five minutes at every change of
horses.   I told him I would not give him two if
I could help it, and would leave him behind as soon
as look at him.   I guess he was smarter in his
movements for the rest of the journey.

The following instructions, issued to the guards
in the same year, seem to point to their having
delivered single letters as they passed through the
villages, but I certainly never saw such a thing done
in later years.   In all the towns there were probably
post-offices, though such things were then few and far
between, not as they are now, in every village.

" You are not to stop at any place to leave letters,
etc., but to blow your horn to give the people notice
that you have got letters for them ; therefore, if they
do not choose to come out to receive them, don't you
get down from your dickey, but take them on, and
bring them back with you on your next journey.
You are ordered by your instructions to blow your
horn when you pass through a town or village.   Be
careful to perform this duty, or I shall be obliged to
punish you."

In the months of January and February, 1795, the
whole country was visited by most serious storms and
floods.   It is described in the post-office minutes as
"dreadful ;" great holes were made in the roads, and

many accidents happened through both coachman and guard being chucked from their boxes, and frequently coaches arrived having lost the guard from that cause. Many bridges were washed away all over the country, of which three alone were between Doncaster and Ferrybridge. The mail coach between Edinburgh and Newcastle took a day longer than usual to do the journey. Nearly all the coaches that attempted to perform their journeys had to take circuitous routes on account of floods. Bridges were washed away, roads rendered impassable by great holes in them, and, in Scotland and the north of England, blocked by snow. In the south, a fast thaw set in, which suddenly changed to intense cold, leaving roads simply sheets of ice. Through the combined exertions of the postmasters, a large number of whom were also mail contractors, many of the roads were cleared sufficiently to admit of the coaches running, but it was months before the mails began to arrive with punctuality, and many mail coach routes had to be altered on account of the roads and bridges not being repaired. This was owing, in most instances, to the road commissioners and local authorities failing to come to settlement in supplying the money for the work to be done, and in many instances the Postmaster-General was compelled to indict them for neglecting to put the road in good repair. The guards suffered very much from the intense cold and dampness, and many were allowed, in addition to the half-guinea per week wages, a further half-guinea, as, on account of their having no passengers to carry, they received no " vails." All their doctors' bills were paid, and the following are but a few of the many guards who received rewards for the manner in which they performed their duty.

John Rees, guard from Swansea to Bristol, who, in consequence of the waters being so rapid, was obliged to proceed by horse, when near Bridgend, was up to his shoulders, and in that condition, in the night, did not wait to change his clothes, but proceeded on his duty ; was awarded one guinea.

Thomas Sweatman, guard to the Chester mail, was obliged to alight from his mail box at Hockliffe to fix the bars and put on some traces, up to his hips in water in the middle of the night, after which it froze severely, and he came in that condition to London ; awarded half a guinea.

John Jelfs rode all the way from Cirencester to Oxford, and Oxford to Cirencester through snow and water, the coach not being able to proceed ; awarded five shillings.

To our modern notions, the post-office authorities hardly erred on the side of liberality, but half a guinea was thought much more of in those days.

CHAPTER II.

THE ROYAL MAILS (*continued*).

By the beginning of the new century the mail coach system appears to have begun to settle into its place pretty well. Mr. Vidler had the contract for the coaches, which he continued to hold for at least a quarter of a century, and appears to have brought much spirit to bear upon the work.

In the year 1820 he was evidently engaged in making experiments with the view of making the coaches run lighter after the horses, and also to test their stability. He writes to Mr. Johnson, the Superintendent of mail coaches, May 15, saying, "As below, I send you the particulars of an experiment made this morning with a mail coach with the five hundredweight in the three different positions," and he accompanied this letter with cards, of which I give an exact copy.

Post Coach.	Mail.
77 lbs. to remove with 5 cwt. on front wheels.	70 lbs. to remove with 5 cwt. on front wheels.
74 lbs. to remove with 5 cwt. on hind wheels.	65 lbs. to remove with 5 cwt. on hind wheels.
68 lbs. to remove with 5 cwt. in centre of the coach.	61 lbs. to remove with 5 cwt. in centre of coach.

Mail	Balloon.
56 lbs. suspended over a pulley moved the mail on a horizontal plane. Weight 18 cwt. 20 lbs. Fore wheels 3 feet 8 inches. Hind wheels 4 feet 6 inches. The fore wheel raised on a block, stood at 26 inches without upsetting.	It required 60 lbs. to move the Balloon. Weight 18 cwt. 1 qr. 19 lbs. Fore wheels 3 feet 6 inches. Hind wheels 4 feet 10 inches. The fore wheel of the Balloon would only stand at 17. The hind at $16\frac{1}{2}$.

Double-bodied Coach with Fore and Hind Boot.

Weight 14 cwt. Fore wheels 3 feet 8 inches. Hind wheels 4 feet 6 inches. 28 lbs. suspended over a pulley moved this coach on a horizontal plane. The fore and hind wheels raised on blocks at 31 inches did not upset the coach.	It required only 35 lbs. to move this coach with 5 cwt. in front boot. 32 lbs. to move it with 5 cwt. in the hind boot. $33\frac{1}{4}$ lbs. to move it with 5 cwt. in the centre of the body.

I confess I am not expert enough to quite understand all this, but I have been induced to place it before the reader, as it occupies little space, and may be of interest to those who have a practical acquaintance with mechanics. I am equally at a loss to say what sort of conveyance the Balloon or the Double-bodied Coach were.

The Postmaster-General, and those under him, appear to have always been ready to listen to any proposals or suggestions made to them for the improvement of coaches, even if, as in the case below, they were not very promising.

In the year 1811, the Rev. Mr. Milton tried to persuade the Postmaster-General to adopt a system of broad wheels to save the roads, and got it adopted by a Reading coach ; but, as might be expected, it was found to add immensely to the draught, and is described as being the only coach which distressed the horses. The rev. gentleman must have been a commissioner of some turnpike trust, and had imbibed such a predilection for broad wheels for the sake of the roads, that he resembled the tanner, who affirmed that " there was nothing like leather."

Even without the wheels being broad, the difference between square tires and round tires is enormous. This was brought to my notice very strongly one summer when the round tires which were worn out were replaced by square ones. The difference to the horses in the draught was considerable, but it was most striking when going down hill, where the change made the difference of a notch or two in the brake.

But, without having broad wheels, coaches were by far the best customers the roads had. They paid large sums of money, and really benefited the roads, rather than injured them. A road is more easily kept in repair when it has a variety of traffic over it. When, as is commonly the case now, it is nearly all

single horse work, the wheels and the horses always
keep to the same tracks, and the new metal requires
constant raking to prevent the road getting into ruts ;
whereas, with a variety in the traffic, the stone settles
with little trouble.

Probably little or no alteration took place in the
build of the mail coaches during Mr. Vidler's contract,
but at the expiration of it the telegraph spring, the
same as was at work under the other coaches, was
substituted for what was termed the mail coach spring,
which had hitherto been in use as the hind spring.
This alteration had the desirable effect of shortening
the perch, which was favourable to draught, and, at the
same time, it let down the body, which was of a
square build, lower down between the springs, which
added to the stability. The same axles and wheels
were continued, only that the tires, instead of being
put on in "stocks," were like those on other coach
wheels fastened on in one circle.

As late, however, as the year 1839, the post-office
authorities did not appear to be quite satisfied, as an
enquiry was instituted; but I cannot find that any
change of much value was suggested, and certainly
none was the outcome of the enquiry. A Mr. J.
M'Neil, in his evidence, said that there was no
reason why, if the front part of the carriage was
upon telegraph springs, the hind part should not be
upon C springs. This, no doubt, would check the

swing attendant upon the C spring, but might give a rather rude shock to the telegraph spring in doing so.

Four years later I find that the sum of thirty shillings was allowed for "drawing the pattern of a coach." The plan, however, was not forthcoming.

The following statement shows how large the business of the mail coach department had become by the year 1834, just half a century after its establishment. In England alone the number of miles travelled daily by mail coaches was 16,262. The amount of expense for forwarding the mails was £56,334; amount of mail guards' wages £6,743; the number of them employed was 247; the number of roads on which the coachman acted as guard was 34; the number of roads on which the patent coaches were used was 63, and on which not used was 51. The patent coaches, therefore, seem to have been brought into use slowly.

MILEAGE WARRANTS (October, 1834).

3 at 1d.	1 at 3½d.
1 „ 1¼d.	1 „ 4d.
34 „ 1½d.	3 paid yearly sums.
42 „ 2d.	1 received no pay.
4 „ 3d.	

Perhaps I shall find no better place than this for

introducing the reader more intimately to the mail
guards. It will be seen that their numbers were very
considerable, and as they had exceedingly onerous
and responsible duties to perform (and that sometimes
at the risk of their lives), and were the servants of
the post-office, it would naturally have been expected
that they should have been well paid. All that they
received, however, from the post-office was ten
shillings and sixpence a week and one suit of clothes,
in addition to which they were entitled to a
superannuation allowance of seven shillings a week,
and frequently received assistance in iilness. For
the rest they had to trust to the tips given to them
by the passengers, and I think it speaks well for the
liberality of the travelling public that they were
satisfied with their places; for having post-office duty
to perform in every town they passed through, they
could have had little opportunity to confer any
benefits upon them.

On the subject of fees, too, their employers blew
hot and cold. At one time, as has been observed,
they made them an allowance for the loss of "vails";
and at another, as will be seen by the accompanying
letter, the practice was condemned. A complaint had
been received from a passenger respecting fees to
coachmen and guards; but the letter will speak for
itself.

"I have the honour of your letter, to which I beg

leave to observe that neither coachman nor guard should claim anything of 'vails' as a right, having ten and sixpence per week each ; but the custom too much prevailed of giving generally each a shilling at the end of the ground, but as a courtesy, not a right ; and it is the absolute order of the office that they shall not use a word beyond solicitation. This is particularly strong to the guard, for, indeed, over the coachman we have not much power ; but if he drives less than thirty miles, as your first did, they should think themselves well content with sixpence from each passenger." It goes on to say that the guard was suspended for his conduct.

I don't know how far coachmen were contented with sixpence in those days ; but I know that so small a sum, if offered, would have given little satisfaction in later years, if not returned with thanks.

It will still be in the recollection of a good many that in the early days of railways the mail bags were only forwarded by a certain number of trains, which were called mail trains, and were in charge of a post-office guard. They may also call to mind that there used to be attached to those trains some carriages a good deal resembling the old mail coaches, and constructed to carry only four passengers in each compartment. So difficult is it to break altogether with old associations.

The guards were then placed on what was termed the treasury list, and their salary was raised to seventy pounds a year and upwards.

Before I pass on from the subject of the guards, I should like to put once again before the reader the onerous and, indeed, dangerous nature of their duties, and the admirable and faithful way in which they performed them. Among other reports of the same nature I have selected the following, which occurred in November, 1836 :—

"The guard, Rands, a very old servant, on the Ludlow and Worcester line, states the coach and passengers were left at a place called Newnham, in consequence of the water being too deep for the coach to travel. I took the mail on horseback until I could procure a post chaise to convey the bags to meet the mail for London. This lost one hour and fourteen minutes, but only forty-five minutes' delay on the arrival in London."

Out of their very moderate pay, those of them working out of London, and in Ireland, were called upon to pay the sum of six shillings and sixpence quarterly to the armourer for cleaning arms, but in the country they looked after their own. How far these were kept in serviceable order I have no means of knowing, but judging from a very strange and melancholy accident which occurred in Ireland, those in charge of the armourers appear to have been kept in very fit condition for use, indeed, if not rather too much so. The report says, "As the Sligo mail was preparing to start from Ballina, the guard, Samuel Middleton, was in the act of closing the lid of his arm chest, when, unfortunately, a blunderbuss exploded, one of the balls from which entered the side of a poor country-man, name Terence M'Donagh, and caused his in-stant death." If this had occurred now, I suppose, by some reasoning peculiarly Hibernian, this accident would have been laid at Mr. Balfour's door.

As has been shown by the mileage warrant the remuneration paid to the coach proprietors for horsing the mails was, with the exception of two or three cases, always very small. How they contrived to make any profit out of it, with at first only four passengers, is to me a mystery. I can only suppose that the fares charged to the passengers were very high. As the roads improved, and the conveyances were made more comfortable and commodious, three outside passengers were allowed to be carried, and the pace being accelerated, no doubt many of the mails had a pretty good time of it till the roads were suffi-ciently improved for the fast day coaches to commence running. Up to this time the only competition they experienced was that of the slow and heavy night coaches, and all the "*élite*," who did not object to pay well for the improved accommodation, travelled by the mails, which were performing their journeys

at a good speed considering the then condition of
the roads.

In the year 1811, according to a table in the edition of " Patterson's Roads," published in that year, the
mail from London to Chester and Holyhead, which
started from the General Post Office at eight o'clock
on Monday evening, arrived at Chester at twenty-five
minutes past twelve on the morning of the following
Wednesday, thus taking about twenty-eight hours and
a half to perform a journey of one hundred and eighty
miles. The "Bristol" occupied fifteen hours and three-
quarters on her journey of one hundred and twenty
miles, whilst that to Shrewsbury, which at that time
ran by Uxbridge and Oxford, consumed twenty-three
hours in accomplishing the distance of one hundred
and sixty-two miles, and, as Nimrod remarked in his
article on the Road, " Perhaps, an hour after her time
by Shrewsbury clock." This shows a speed of nearly
eight miles an hour, which, if kept, was very credit-
able work ; but upon this we see that Nimrod casts a
doubt, and he adds " The betting were not ten to one
that she had not been overturned on the road."

By the year 1825, some considerable acceleration
had taken place. The Shrewsbury mail, which had
then become the more important Holyhead mail, performed the journey to Shrewsbury in twenty hours
and a half, and was again accelerated in the following
year, but to how great an extent I have no know-

ledge. I only know that a few years later the time
allowed was reduced to sixteen hours and a quarter,
and she was due at Holyhead about the same time as,
a few years previously, she had reached Shrewsbury,
or twenty-eight hours from London; and thus,
owing in a great degree to the admirable efficiency
of Mr. Telford's road-making, surpassing by six
hours the opinion expressed by him in the year
1830, that the mail ought to go to Holyhead in
thirty-four hours. The remuneration paid to the
horse contractors was, with very few exceptions,
always very small, as the table already introduced
shows.

Notwithstanding all the improvements in the mails,
however, when the fast day coaches became their
rivals, they more and more lost their good customers
and then began the complaints about the small amount
paid by the post-office. So much, indeed, did this
competition tell, that when the Shrewsbury mail
became the Holyhead, and changed its route from the
Oxford road to that through Coventry, the contractors
would accept no less than a shilling a mile, fearing
the opposition they would have to meet by those who
had lost the mail on the other road. It was, however,
largely reduced afterwards, but to what extent I have
not ascertained; and again, upon an acceleration in
1826, it was increased to fourpence, with the proviso
that if it shared less than four pounds a mile per

month during the ensuing year, the price should be raised to fivepence.

The Chester mail also obtained a rise to sixpence at the same time, as it did not earn four pounds a mile ; doubtless in consequence of its having ceased to carry the Holyhead traffic.

The dissatisfaction of the contractors appears to have continued, and, indeed, became more intense as the coaches improved and multiplied, till at last a committee of the House of Commons was appointed to investigate the circumstances, which, however, I should have thought were not very far to seek ; but at any rate, it elicited some good, sound, common sense from Mr. Johnson, the superintendent of mail coaches.

He was of opinion that anything under fivepence a mile was too little, and that mail coaches which received less than that were decidedly underpaid. Still the competition was so great that persons were generally found to undertake the contract for less ; but he did not desire to bring forward persons to take it at less than threepence a mile, as it would be injurious to them if they excited that sort of opposition. He considered that a dividend of four pounds a mile a month was sufficient to cover loss, but with scarcely sufficient profit. Indeed, fast coaches ought to share five, and I can quite bear him out in this.

He was, evidently, a very sensible, practical man,

and knew that innkeepers would be found to horse mails for almost nothing, merely for the sake of the prestige which attached to them, the increased custom they brought to the bar, and old rivalry, which was often exceedingly strong, and he preferred to pay a fair sum to be sure and keep responsible men.

He considered that mails, on account of the limited number of passengers, worked at a disadvantage when opposed by other coaches ; and no doubt he was right, because if a coach carrying fifteen or sixteen passengers was nearly empty to-day, it would be remunerated by a full load to-morrow ; whereas, the mail with only seven, when full, could not be reimbursed by one good load. It required to be pretty evenly loaded every day to make it pay.

He said a majority of our mail coaches are not earning what is considered the minimum remuneration for a public carriage.

He considered that to run toll free and duty free was sufficient to secure them against competition, but, curiously enough, this never seems to have been tried, for though the roads were compelled to let the mails run without paying toll, the Chancellor of the Exchequer always claimed the mileage duty, which was twopence a mile. There was also a duty of five pounds for the stage-coach licence, or what was termed the plates, which they were obliged to carry. The mails, however, were excused from carrying the plates, as it was said His

Majesty's mails ought not to be disfigured; but whether
they enjoyed the more substantial benefit of having
the five pounds remitted I have not been able to
ascertain.

As time went on, and fast coaches increased, Mr.
Johnson must have been at his wit's end to know how
to get the mail bags carried. Mail carts appear to
have been an expensive luxury, as they cost a shilling
a mile, and he could generally do better with the
coach proprietors.

In some cases there was so much difficulty in filling
up stages that it was repeatedly necessary to send
orders that if no horses were to be found to take the
coach over a certain stage, to forward it by post
horses.

The Norwich mail, through Newmarket, received
eightpence a mile, of which two hundred pounds
seems to have been advanced to help the proprietors
out of difficulties, and to induce them to go on at all;
but that mail was very strongly opposed by an excellent day coach, the " Norwich Telegraph," from the
"Golden Cross," Charing Cross.

So little at this time was the post-office work
valued where it interfered with the hours or increased
the pace, that a night coach on the same Norwich road
as the mail declined to compete, and it was suggested,
but not carried out, to put a guard upon a coach,
making a contract with him to carry the letters, giving

them some advantage for so doing, which would make it worth their while ; and a coach at one time was employed to carry the bags between Alton and Gosport, which were brought to the former place by the Poole mail.

It did not, however, meet with Mr. Johnson's approval. He says, " I think that the use of coaches in that way goes directly to destroy the regular mail coach system. I think that if any coach from London to Manchester were to be allowed to carry ten outsides, it never would arrive within an hour of the present mail coach, from the interruption which is occasioned by the number of outside passengers, not to speak of the insecurity of the bags."

No doubt he was quite right, as a rule ; but if he lived to witness the " Telegraph " coach perform with regularity that journey of one hundred and eighty-six miles in eighteen hours, he would have confessed that there might be exceptions to the rule.

He says, speaking generally of the system, with a justifiable spice of *esprit de corps*, " I think we should look to the general result of the mail coach system, and that we should provide the best expedient we can for cases of difficulty. If we employed such coaches we could not prevent the parties from writing Royal Mail Coach upon them, and writing Royal Mail Coach Office upon all their establishments in the towns where they reside ; all of which would go very much to destroy the distinction by which the present mail coaches greatly depend, and we should consider that after the mail coach system has supplied all the uses of the post-office, it is still valuable as a national system. It originally set the example of that travelling which is so much admired, not only at home, but even throughout Europe, and I hope continues to set an example now. I am persuaded that the manner in which the stage coaches have been accelerated arose entirely from their desire to rival the mails upon their old plan, and they now try to keep as close to them as they can, though, in all long distances, they are certainly very far behind. Persons of the first distinction travel by the mail coaches. I don't mean amateur whips, but persons who depend upon the regularity, security, and comfort of the mail coach, and being less likely to meet with disagreeable passengers."

He adds, "I am not aware of any coach that goes as fast as the mail for a hundred and fifty miles, not even the 'Wonder,' and if some days as fast, they are able, whenever they think proper, to relax their speed, which the mail, being under contract, cannot do."

The keen competition between the mails and other coaches is well emphasized by a letter written by Mr. Spencer, the coach proprietor at Holyhead, to Mr. Chaplin in London, complaining that as the "Nimrod" had commenced running through to Holyhead, they were obliged to carry passengers at lower fares, and saying that he had by that night's mail booked a lady through to London, inside, for four pounds; and from my own experience, I can quite believe this, as some of the ladies of the Principality are like Mrs. Gilpin, who, though on pleasure bent, had a frugal mind.

When I was driving the "Snowdonian" upon one up journey, upon looking at the "way-bill," as I left Dolgelly, I perceived that there was a lady booked, to be taken up a mile or two out of the town, to go a short distance, the fare for which was three shillings and sixpence "*to pay.*" She took her place in the coach in due course, and having alighted at her destination, I demanded her fare from her, upon which she assured me that she could only pay half-a-crown, as she had no more money with her. I told her that I was responsible for the full fare, and that she really must pay it; and when she saw that I was determined to have no nonsense about it, she asked me if I could give her change for a sovereign, to which I replied, "Yes, or two, if you like;" whereupon, she opened her purse and exposed to my delighted eyes two or three shiners.

But to show how serious was the reduction made by the Holyhead mail, it will be sufficient to say that the fares by the Edinburgh mail, which ran a distance of only one hundred and thirty miles more, were eleven guineas and a half inside, and seven and a half outside : a full way-bill amounting to sixty-eight

guineas and a half.   Now this, with fees to coachmen,
guards, and porters, would make a journey to the
northern capital from the southern one cost about
fourteen pounds for an inside passenger, and about
ten for one travelling outside, and it occupied forty
hours.

The distance may now be performed in nine hours
and at a cost of two pounds, or less by Parliamentary
train.

We have seen the mail bags no heavier than could
be carried by a boy riding a pony, but before the
railway system commenced they had increased to such
an extent that some mail coaches could carry no more,
and, in two cases, they required to be subsidised.
For some time the "Greyhound," Shrewsbury coach,
was paid every Saturday night for two outside places
to Birmingham, in consideration of their carrying two
mail bags as far as that town· on account of the
number of newspapers ; and when that coach ceased
running the Holyhead mail was paid for outside places
to enable them to dispense with that number of
passengers, and find the extra space required for these
bags.   The Dover mail also received assistance in
the form of an extra coach once a week for the
foreign, or what were called the black bags, as they
were dressed with tar to render them waterproof.

With this before me I cannot help asking myself
whether it was not somewhat of a leap in the dark to

reduce the postage at one bound from the existing high rates to one penny. If the railways had not been constructed with the celerity they were, there must have been great difficulty and increased expenses in conveying the mails, as it would have been impossible for the mail coaches to carry them and passengers as well. I suppose, however, we must conclude that Sir Rowland Hill had, with great foresight, and much consideration, assured himself that such would be the case with the railways, and that he might safely trust to their rapid development and co-operation for carrying out his great project. Though the result might not have been equally clear to others as to himself, he was only like the great engineer, George Stephenson, who, when examined before a Committee of the House of Commons, for the sake of humouring the distrust and nervousness of his interrogators, placed the speed at which he expected the trains to travel at ten miles an hour, though, at the same time he quite reckoned upon, at least, double that speed.

The mail coaches working out of London had a gala day every year. On the King's birthday they all paraded, spick and span, with the coaches new or else freshly painted and varnished, the coachmen and guards wearing their new scarlet liveries, picked teams with new harness, and rosettes in their heads : blue and orange ones in old George the Third's day ; but the orange, for some cause or other, was changed to red in the succeeding reign. In this form they formed up and paraded through several of the principal thorough-fares at the West End, returning to their respective yards preparatory to the serious business of the night.

It was a very pretty pageant, but there was another scene connected with them, and which, to my mind, was quite, if not more interesting, which could be witnessed every week-day evening in St. Martin's-le-Grand, between the hours of half-past seven and eight. Soon after the former hour all the mail coaches—with the exception of seven or eight, which left London by the western roads, and received their bags at the " White Horse Cellar," or "Gloucester Coffee-house," to which places they were taken in mail carts—began to arrive at the General Post Office to receive their bags. They turned into the yard, through the gateway nearest to Cheapside, and took up their places behind the building in a space which has been very much encroached upon since by buildings, and, as eight o'clock struck, they were to be seen emerging through the lower gateway, and turning off on their respective routes, spreading out like a sky rocket as they advanced into the country.

During the long days in summer they turned out nearly as smart as upon the Royal birthday, but on a dark, stormy blustering evening in December or January, when snow or rain were falling steadily, there was an appearance of business, and very serious business about them. The scarlet coats were obscured from view by the somewhat elaborate upper coats which have been elsewhere described; and there was a feeling of serious reality about the whole thing, not unlike that which comes over one upon seeing a ship start on a long voyage, or a regiment embarking for foreign service. One felt that they would probably meet with more or less difficulty, or, at any rate, that there was an arduous task before them. The horses would be changed, the coachmen would be changed, the guards would be changed, probably there would be a considerable change in the passengers, but the wheels roll on for ever, or, at any rate, till they arrive at their journey's end, which, in some cases, would extend not only through that night, but continue till darkness again returned, when the same work went on through another night, and in two or three instances was not concluded till the sun was again high in the heavens; and so admirably was the service performed that the betting was long odds in favour of each coach reaching its destination at the correct time.

They had to contend not only with climatic influences, but sometimes the malice of man placed stumbling-blocks in their way. The same diabolical

spirit which induces men at the present time to place
obstructions across the permanent way of railways,
led some miscreants in November, 1815, to place
several gates at night right across the road near
Warrington, which caused the guard of the Leicester
mail to get down ten times to remove them, and, but
for the moonlight, would have caused serious accidents,
and a cart was also fixed across the road. Gates were
also, on a subsequent occasion, placed on the road
near Stockton to catch the Chester mail. The
perpetrators of these wanton outrages do not appear
to have been discovered, or they would doubtless
have met with their deserts, as the Postmaster-
General was armed with large powers for protecting
and preventing delay to the mails. Among other
convictions for interrupting the free passage of the
mails, one toll-gate man near Henley is recorded to
have been fined fifty shillings, and also different
carters in sums up to thirty shillings. An innkeeper
was liable to the forfeiture of his licence for such an
offence.

The most trying time for the coachmen and guards
were the two first hours on the road. After that, few
vehicles were moving about, but up to that time a
large number of all sorts, many of which were without
lights, were in motion, and not only was a very careful
look-out by the former necessary, but the latter had
often, especially on thick nights, to make a free use of

his horn to avoid collisions. The roads for the first
ten miles out of town, as far as Barnet to the north
and Hounslow to the west, might, when the days
were not at their longest, be said to be a blaze of
light. Between the down mails leaving London and
the day coaches arriving, none with less than three
lamps, and many with five, and some even with six,
it was a bad look-out for travellers who drove horses
that were frightened at lights. Indeed, I have known
some persons very nervous on this subject. They
seemed to think that because the strong light dazzled
them, it must have the same effect upon the
coachman's eyes ; and, when I have been driving a
coach very strongly lighted, I have known men to
leave the road and drive into a field to get out of my
way. The presence of a number of coaches carrying
powerful lights, and going both ways, probably does
have the tendency of throwing small carriages without
lamps into the shade, and so making it more difficult
to see them. An aspiring costermonger, trying to
thread his way with his donkey and cart among the
numerous other vehicles, might be overlooked without
much difficulty among such a brilliant company.

CHAPTER III.

ACCIDENTS.

I HAVE sometimes been asked, when I was driving coaches, whether I had ever had an accident, to which I was able to reply for a good many years, that, though I had been very near several, I had been fortunate enough to steer clear of them. I had experienced different things which might easily have ended in an accident, such as a leader's rein breaking, the bit falling out of a wheel horse's mouth, a fore wheel coming off, and similar things, but had always managed to pull up without coming to grief. The case of the wheel might have been attended with very serious consequences if we had been going fast at the time, but fortunately it occurred just when I had pulled up to go slowly round a corner.

At last, however, it did come, and I think I may say "with a vengeance," though it was not accompanied with any loss of life or limb, or indeed any very serious consequences. It occurred when I was working the Aberystwith and Caernarvon "Snowdonian." A pole chain broke when descending a rather steep fall of ground, which caused the coach to approach the off-side of the road, and, as the lamps threw their light very high, I did not see a large stone, commonly called in the parlance of the road, " a waggoner," until it was close under the roller bolt, and immediately afterwards the fore wheel struck it with such violence that the concussion threw the box passenger and myself off the box. He was thrown clear of the coach, whilst I was pitched over the wheelers' heads, but, alighting upon the leaders' backs, was quietly let down to the ground between them. This, mercifully, laid me what the sailors call " fore and aft," and consequently the coach was able to pass over without touching me, and beyond a broken arm, I was little the worse. The horses galloped on for a few hundred yards, and then ran the off-side wheels up the hedge-bank, upsetting the coach into the road.

This was somewhat of a lesson to me, for perhaps I had got the horses into the habit of going rather too fast down the falls of ground, of which there were several in the stage, but if I had not made play there, it would have been impossible to keep time. We were horsed by one of the hotel proprietors in Caernarvon, and it was certainly the worst team I ever drove. Underbred to start with, and, though our pace was not fast, yet from age and other infirmities too slow for it even such as it was.

Nevertheless, time was bound to be kept somehow,

as we not unfrequently carried passengers who wanted
to proceed from Caernarvon by the up mail train, and
there was not much time to spare.

There was one thing I never would do, and that
was to call upon good horses, the property of one
proprietor, to fetch up time lost by the bad ones
belonging to another.

I have previously alluded to being near accidents
in consequence of a broken rein, and when I was
driving the Aberystwith and Kington "Cambrian"
I had a very near shave indeed from that cause. We
had just commenced the descent of Radnor forest on
the up journey, and I had begun to "shove 'em along
a bit," when the near lead rein broke, and, consequently,
the leaders got, to use a nautical phrase, athwart the
wheelers. Of course, I tightened the brake at once,
and was able to bring the coach to a standstill before
any harm was done, as the pole held, and the horses
were quiet, but another yard or two more and the
coach must have gone over, as the leaders were already
jammed in between the wheelers and a high hedge
bank, with their heads turned the wrong way.

Perhaps some reader may say, "What a shame it
was to use such reins, they ought not to be able to
break;" and of course they ought not, but horsekeepers
were not the most reliable of men, and no coachman
could possibly find time to examine the harness at
every stage. If leading reins could be cut out of one

J.Sturgess del. et lith.

M&N.Hanhart imp

HORSES IN A HEAP. LEADER DOWN, WHEELERS FALLING OVER HIM.

length of leather, there would be very few or no breakages, but as they are obliged to be made of several
lengths sewn together, they are liable to break, as they
get old, from the stitches becoming rotten. Nevertheless
such things ought not to happen, but as I knew they
would, I always carried about me two short straps the
same width as the reins, one about two inches long, with
a buckle at both ends, and the other with a buckle at one
end and a billet at the other, so that a breakage would
be easily repaired at whatever part it might occur.

I have twice had three out of the four horses in
a heap, from a leader coming down and the two
wheelers falling over him; but in such a case as this
there is very little danger if the coachman has the
presence of mind not to leave his box till there is
sufficient strength at the horses' heads to prevent
them jumping up and starting off frightened.

These, and a few others which have come to the
front in connection with other subjects, are all the
accidents and close shaves which I have experienced
as a coachman; and when I call to mind the many
thousand miles I have driven, over some very
indifferent roads, with heavy loads, at all hours,
in all weathers, and with all sorts of "*cattle,*" I
think I may consider myself fortunate. But then I
was insured in the "Railway Passengers' Insurance
Company," and recommend all other coachmen to do
the same.

So much for my own experiences. Now for a few which have been gone through by others.

All those which have resulted from climatic influences will be introduced in connection with their respective causes, but I will venture to present to the reader others which, from one cause or another, possess more or less a character of their own, and are distinguished either by extraordinary escapes, great recklessness, or some other remarkable feature. The first I shall notice is distinguished by the singularity of the escapes, and I cannot convey the circumstances connected with it better than by giving the report of the inspector upon the accident which occurred to the Gloucester and Caermarthen mail on December 19, 1835. He says :—

" It appears from the tracks of the wheels, which are still visible, owing to the frost setting in immediately after the accident, that about a hundred yards before the cart was met, the mail was in the middle of the road, leaving room on either side for the cart to pass, and at this distance the cart was seen to be on the wrong side of the road. The coachman called out in the usual way when the carter crossed to his near side of the road, and had the coachman gone to his near side, no accident would have occurred ; but, by the tracks of the wheels, it is quite clear that the coachman took the off-side of the road in a sort of sweep, when the leaders coming in

J. Sturgess del et lith.

WENT OVER BANK & HEDGE .

M&N Hanhart imp.

front of the cart, and not being able to pass, went over the bank and hedge, the latter being low; and then the wheelers followed in as regular a manner as if they had been going down a street, and all the four wheels of the coach went on the bank straight forward and went down the precipice in this manner for some short distance before the mail went over, which it did on the right side, and turned over four times before it was stopped by coming against an oak tree. But for this impediment to its progress it would have turned over again and fallen into a river. The pole was broken at both ends, and the perch and hind springs were broken. The fore boot was left in its progress; the mail box was dashed to atoms, and the luggage and bags strewed in all directions. A tin box containing valuable deeds was broken, and the deeds scattered in all directions, but have been all recovered, and are safe in Colonel Gwynne's possession, to whom they belong. When the coach came against the tree it was on its wheels. Colonel Gwynne caused it to be chained and locked to the tree till the inspector should see it. The distance from the road to the tree is eighty-seven feet. The passengers were Colonel Gwynne on the box, Mr. D. Jones, Mr. Edwards, and Mr. Kenrick on the roof, and Mr. Lloyd Harris and Mr. Church inside. Colonel Gwynne jumped off when he saw the leaders going over the bank, as did Edward Jenkins the coachman and Compton the guard. The latter was somewhat stunned at first, but all escaped with slight hurt.

" Mr. D. Jones was found about half-way down the precipice, bleeding much, having received several cuts about the head and face, and was a good deal bruised and in a senseless state. Mr. Harris, when the coach came in contact with the tree, was forced through the part from which the boot had been separated, and fell into the river. He remembers nothing of the accident except feeling cold when in the river, from which, somehow or other, he got out and went to a farmhouse near, where he was found in a senseless state. He has a severe cut on the upper lip, but both he and Mr. Jones are recovering rapidly. Mr. Kenrick was not hurt in the least. The accident appears to have been one of the most extraordinary ever heard of, and the escape of the passengers with their lives most miraculous. The coachman's conduct seems to have been most censurable. He is reported by the guard and passengers to have driven the whole of the way most irregularly. He was remonstrated with by them, but, as has been seen, with no effect. One of the passengers thought he was drunk, but the guard says he did not observe it, but that he only heard him speak once. The horses were so little injured that they were at work the next day in their usual places."

The coachman was afterwards brought before the magistrates, when he pleaded guilty to negligence and being on the wrong side of the road, and was fined five pounds.

On 13th January, 1836, when the Falmouth and Exeter mail was about three miles from Okehampton, the coachman drove against a heap of stones which had been placed too far out from the off-side of the road, and the concussion was so great that both himself and the guard were thrown off. The horses, finding themselves under no control, immediately went off at a smart pace, and, although they had three sharp turns to take, and a hill to go down, actually arrived at the Okehampton turnpike gate without the slightest accident. There was one gentleman inside, who was not aware that anything was amiss, but merely thought the coachman was driving too fast. Perhaps the despised turnpike gate prevented a serious accident in this case.

In July, 1839, the Ipswich mail, when arriving at Colchester, the coachman Flack, as is usual, threw down the reins and got down when no horsekeeper was at the horses' heads, and they galloped off till the near leader fell and broke his neck, which stopped them. Probably this accident would not have occurred if the coach had been fitted with a brake, which the coachman ought to put on tight before leaving his box.

An old friend of mine writes me, " One night I was a passenger in the Glasgow mail, driven by Captain Baynton, and felt rather uneasy when I found we were racing with the Edinburgh mail for the Stamford Hill toll-gate.   The consequence was, we cannoned in the gate, and a most awful crash ensued, killing two wheel horses and seriously injuring the other two.   It is needless to say that Billy Chaplin never allowed the captain to take the Glasgow mail out of the yard again."   Anything more reckless than this could not possibly be.   Not only were they racing down hill, but the gate was too narrow to admit of both coaches going through abreast ; consequently, unless the nerve of one of the coachmen gave way before it was too late, so as to make him decline the contest in time, a smash was inevitable.   Neither had they the excuse that they were driving opposition coaches.

On September 29th, 1835, when the coachman of the Ipswich mail was getting into his seat at the " Swan with Two Necks " yard in Lad Lane, the horses suddenly started off, knocking down the man who was attending at their heads, and throwing the coachman off the steps.   They then proceeded at a rapid pace into Cheapside, when the coach, catching the hind part of the Poole mail, the concussion was so great that it threw the coachman of that mail from his box with such violence that he was taken up senseless, and was carried to the hospital in a dangerous state. The horses of the Ipswich mail, continuing their speed, ran the pole into the iron railings of the area of Mr. Ripling's house, which breaking, fortunately set the leaders at liberty, when the wheel horses were soon stopped without doing any further damage.

To anyone who remembers the situation of the yard of the " Swan with Two Necks," it will be a matter of surprise how four horses, entirely left to their own guidance, could possibly steer the coach clear of the different corners between it and Cheapside.

The following is an instance of a coach absolutely rolling over.

The " Liverpool Express," when near Chalk Hill on her journey to London, though not a particularly fast coach, was going at a great pace, as the stage was only four miles, and she was making time for a long stage to follow. Somehow or another she got on the rock, which is easily done with a coach heavily loaded on the roof if the wheel horses are not poled up even, or not the right length, and the coach is kept too much on the side of the road.

Though I have elsewhere said a good deal on the subject of pole chains, I have been induced to make a practical application here for the benefit of any young coachmen who may be disposed to spring their

teams on a nice piece of flat ground. But to return
to the " Express."

It was a very old coach, and the transom plate was
so much worn as to have become round, and she
rolled over, killing one passenger and severely injuring
two more. " They were thrown off like a man sowing
wheat broadcast," says my informant. One passenger
brought an action against the proprietors and recovered heavy damages, though they tried to saddle
it on the coachman's driving too fast; but the jury laid
it to the bad state of the transom plate, and gave
damages accordingly.

The following accident, like many others, is one
which ought not to have happened at all, and it
appears to me that, after all the investigation which
took place, the saddle was put upon the back of the
wrong horse. However, I will give the Post-office
minute upon the occasion :—

" London and Worcester mail coach accident
caused through carrying an extra passenger on the
box, July 9th, 1838.

" As the mail coach was entering Broadway, the
horses ran away; when the leading reins breaking,
the coach was drawn against a post, and the pole and
splinter bar were broken. Fortunately, the coach did
not overturn. The reason for the horses taking fright
could not be ascertained, but the guard stated that
the book-keeper at Oxford had insisted on placing an

extra passenger on the box seat with the coachman, who had declared since the accident that, if the extra passenger had not been on the box seat, he would have been enabled to stop the horses.

"An order was issued that the book-keeper and coachman were to be summoned, with the intent of punishing them both with the utmost rigour of the law ; as regards the coachman for allowing an extra person to ride with him, and the book-keeper for insisting that the coachman (who was in a manner obliged to obey his orders) should carry the passenger on the seat with him.

"The inspector found, when applying for the summons, that he could only proceed against the coachman. The case was heard before the magistrates at Oxford, when the coachman was fined in the penalty of fifty shillings and costs."

The question was raised as to asking the contractor to dismiss the coachman, but the opinion of the Postmaster-General was that the punishment had fallen on the wrong man, and he would, therefore, not insist upon his dismissal.

I should have supposed that, in such a case as this, the guard would have had power to summarily prevent an extra passenger being carried. If he had not that power he surely ought to have had it, and if he did possess it, and did not exercise it, he alone was to blame. But, after all, it is difficult to understand how the presence of a third person on the box could have contributed to the breaking of the reins, which was the ultimate cause of the accident.

Amongst the other old institutions and customs which I have raked up from the dust-heap of time, is the law of Deodand, and I will now, by means of an accident, give a practical insight into the working of it.

As the Holyhead mail was one day galloping down a sharp pitch in the road at Shenley, three boys on their way to school, as was a not uncommon practice with boys in those days, tried which of them could run across the road nearest to the horses' heads of the coach. Two of them got across in time and escaped without harm, but the third, being foolhardy, tried to return; the lamentable result of which was that the near side leading bar struck him and knocked him down, causing the mail to run over him, and he was killed on the spot.

A coroner's inquest was held, before which the coachman had to appear, but no blame was attached to him, although a deodand of one sovereign was levied on the coach.

The law appears to have worked hardly in this case. If any one was to blame, it must have been the coachman, and it was rather rough on the proprietors to fine them indirectly for an accident over which they could have no control.

There was a coach from Cambridge to London, called the " Star," what was called an up and down coach ; that is, leaving Cambridge in the morning, and returning again in the evening, from the " Belle Sauvage," Ludgate Hill, which was driven by Joe Walton, a very steady, good coachman, but which, nevertheless, met with a very serious and expensive accident.

Sir St. Vincent Cotton, well known afterwards on the Brighton road, whenever he travelled by the " Star," was allowed by Mr. Nelson, the London pro- prietor, to waggon it, and it was considered a great piece of condescension on the part of old Joe to give up the ribbons to anyone ; but the baronet was a first- rate amateur, and a liberal tipper, so he waived the etiquette. On one of these occasions the " Star " was a little behind time, and St. Vincent was making it up by springing the team a little too freely, which set the coach on the rock, and old Joe becoming nervous, seized hold of the near side reins and thus threw her over. Calloway, the jockey, who was on the coach, had his leg broken, and the accident altogether cost the proprietors nearly two thousand pounds. Sir St. Vincent was unable to assist them much, as he was hard-up at the time.

Probably the fact of the coach being driven by an amateur was not without its effect upon the costs, as, whether he was to blame or not, a jury would not be unlikely to arrive at the conclusion that he was the wrong man in the wrong place.

And now I will wind up this formidable chapter of accidents with one which indicates that the palmy days were passing away, and as it is always somewhat painful to witness the decay of anything one has been fond of, I will draw the veil over the decadence of a system which arrived nearer to perfection than any other road travelling that was ever seen in the world. Sufficient to say that my own experience on a journey during that winter on the Holyhead mail quite confirms the description given of the state of the horses and harness.

I was on the box of the mail one night in the month of January in that winter, when I saw the old short Tommy, which had lain so long on the shelf, reproduced, to enable time to be kept, and in one place there lay by the side of the road the carcase of a horse which had fallen in the up mail. Perhaps it was not very much to be wondered at that the proprietors should be unwilling to go to the expense of buying fresh horses at such a time, but they carried their prudence so far that it partook of cruelty.

The mail coach minute of the General Post Office says : " Collision between the Holyhead mail coach and the Manchester mail coach, 29 June, 1838, at Dirty House Hill, between Weedon and Foster's Booth."

" Both coachmen were in fault. The Holyhead coach had no lamps, and the explanation of their absence was that 28th June of that year was the Coronation Day of our beloved Queen, and the crowd was so great in Birmingham that, in paying attention to getting the horses through the streets, and having lost considerable time in so doing, in the hurry to get the coach off again, the guard did not ascertain if the lamps were with the coach or not. The Manchester coach, at the time of the accident, was attempting, when climbing the hill, to pass the Carlisle mail coach, and was ascending on the wrong side of the road. The horses dashed into each other, with the result that one of the wheel horses of the Holyhead mail, belonging to Mr. Wilson, of Daventry, was killed, and the others injured, one of the leaders seriously. The harness was old, and snapped like chips, or more serious would have been the consequences. In fact, the horse killed was old and worn-out, otherwise, the sudden concussion might have deprived the passengers of life, and, probably, more horses would have been killed. As it was difficult to decide which of the two coachmen was most in the wrong, it was left to the two coachmasters to arrange affairs between themselves."

How the Holyhead, the Manchester, and the Carlisle mails ever got together on the same road I am unable to say, but can only suppose that the rail-

way being open at that time from Liverpool and
Manchester to Birmingham, the bags were in some
way handed over to them for conveyance as far as
was possible, and were then consigned at the terminus
at Birmingham to their respective mail coaches ; but,
even then, I should have thought that the weight of
the bags could not have been sufficient to necessitate
a separate coach for each place.

CHAPTER IV.

COMBATING WITH SNOW, FOGS, AND FLOODS.

How vividly do these words recall the many wet and snowy journeys which I have experienced, both as coachman and passenger, in years gone by, and, strange as it may appear to most people now-a-days, with no unpleasurable associations, though no doubt it was rather trying at the time. Snowstorms, in particular, were very detrimental to coachmen's eyes, particularly when accompanied with high winds. A good look out forward could on no account be relaxed, and that placed the eyes in such a position as was most favourable for the large flakes to fall into them. One coachman on the Holyhead mail, I forget his name, lost his sight from the effects of a snowstorm in the pass of Nant Francon, but probably his eyes had already been weakened by previous experiences of the same nature. I don't think my own have even quite recovered the effects of three winters over the base of Cader Idris.

But, notwithstanding all the bad weather I have been exposed to, I cannot call to mind having ever

5

been wet through outside a coach ; but then I always took care to be well protected by coats, and all other contrivances for withstanding it. I have, however, seen a fellow-passenger, when he dismounted from a coach at the end of an eighty miles' journey, performed in soaking rain, whose boots were as full of water from the rain having run down him, as if he had just walked through a brook.

I never had the misfortune of being regularly snowed up, though I have had some experience of snowdrifts. One of the winters that I drove the "Harkaway" was accompanied by a good deal of snow, and the road for part of the journey, which ran over high and exposed ground, became drifted up, preventing the coach running for two days.

On the third, however, as a slight thaw had set in, it was determined to try and force a way through, especially as the road surveyor had sent some men to clear away the snow. As far as the coach road was concerned, however, these men might nearly as well have stayed at home, as they had confined their attention to letting off the water where it had melted, and when the coach arrived at the spot the drifts remained very much as they had been. Under these circumstances, instead of the proverbial three courses there were only two offered to us—namely, to " go at it or go home." I chose the former alternative, and, catching the horses fast by the head, sent them at the first drift with such a will, that, between the force of the pace and a struggle or two besides, the coach was landed about half way through, when it stuck fast. The workmen now came to our assistance, and dug us out, and I had then only to do the same at the other two drifts, and we managed to catch a train at Machynlleth, though not the right one, as it had taken us two hours to cover a distance of one mile and a half.

Though I have always been fortunate enough to keep clear of dangerous floods, I did so once only by a detour of seven miles, thereby lengthening the day's drive to one hundred, and this reminds me of a rather droll request that was once made to me.

I was driving my drag with a party going to a picnic, and in the course of the drive we had to ford a river which had risen very considerably from the rains of the previous night. When we had got about half-way across, the water had become deep enough to rise a foot or so up the leaders' sides, and the spray was dashing over their backs. Of course, there was nothing to be done except to push on, but a lady called to me from behind, begging me either to turn round, or else put her down. If I had acceded to her last request, she would have met with a cool reception!

Notwithstanding all that was done by the great improvement made in roads, together with the superior class of horses employed and the general

excellence of the coachmen, nothing could be effected
to prevent loss of time or accidents occurring through
severe snows, floods, and fogs, and the mail-bags were
from these causes delayed, although, as we have
already seen, almost superhuman efforts were made
by the guards to get them through the stoppages.

Neither were the Postmaster-General and his
subordinates wanting in using all the means in their
power, whether by expenditure of money or in any
other way, to secure the safety and punctuality of the
mails. The expenses incurred during serious snows,
in paying for the removal of the snow or for extra
horses to the coaches, were considerable. In one
heavy snowstorm the sum of one hundred and ninety
pounds was paid for these purposes, and for another
the cost was one hundred and sixty.

At one time the attention of the Postmaster-
General was called to a snow-plough, and the following circular was issued in December, 1836, to
the postmasters : " I send you some copies of a
description of snow-plough, which has been used with
great advantage in former seasons for the purpose
of forcing a passage through the snow, and I have
to request that you will communicate with the
magistrates, commissioners, trustees, and surveyors
of roads, or other influential persons, urging their
co-operation in endeavouring to remove the im-
pediments to the progress of the mails. The

Postmaster-General relies on all possible efforts being made by yourself and others to secure this important object, and I would suggest whether, among other methods, the passage of the mail coaches through the snow might not be facilitated by placing them on sledges." Whether any pattern of snow-plough or sledge accompanied this missive is not clear, but, judging from some correspondence on the subject, I should fancy there was.

Nothing appears to have been done with either implement, and, indeed, it is not very likely that they would have been popular with the horse contractors. If the snow-ploughs had succeeded in clearing a space sufficient to permit of the passage of a coach, it would probably have left the road in a very heavy state, and I should doubt whether in the climate of this country sledges would have been found of much use. Our frosts are seldom intense enough, and too frequently accompanied with thaws, to allow of the surface being in a fit state for their use for sufficient length of time to make it worth while adapting the coaches to them. If sledges had been brought into general use, probably a good many proprietors would have followed the example set them by one of their number, who, when the coachman had succeeded by great exertions in getting his coach through the snow, said to him, " Why don't you stick her ? " and, strange to relate, she did stick in a drift on the next journey.

Dense fogs, although not altogether stopping the traffic on the roads, were more conducive to accidents than heavy snows, which did absolutely prohibit progress.   In the latter case, at the worst, conveyances were reduced to a complete standstill, and there was an end of it for the time ; but if the fog was of such a density as to be capable of being cut with a knife and fork an attempt must be made.   Though we hear from time to time of all traffic being stopped in the streets of the metropolis, I never recollect to have known of coaches being quite reduced to that state of helplessness ; and, here again, the Postmaster-General is found providing what remedy he could.   In November, 1835, he ordered links to be prepared, but with the assistance of those, even if carried by men on horseback, only very slow progress could have been effected.   It is one of the greatest evils attendant on a fog that it renders lamps useless, and very much circumscribes the light thrown by a link.

If the fog was not very thick indeed, it was possible, though it might be attended by some little risk, to keep going pretty well, but when it became so dense as to hide the horses from the coachman's view there would be no travelling beyond a foot's pace. One could keep pushing along pretty well, as I recollect having done myself when driving a mail, and time had to be kept if at all possible, as long as the hedges could be distinguished, though I hardly knew how soon my leaders would be in the middle of a lot of loose horses which I could not see, but distinctly hear clattering along just in front of us.

Notwithstanding all the care that could be taken, accidents were the inevitable result of the attempts made to keep going, of which I will now give one or two instances, though they were not of a serious nature.

On December 3rd, 1839, the Gloucester and Stroud mails, which ran for a long distance over the same ground, were both drawn off the road and upset in a thick fog, and within a few days of this occurrence the Edinburgh mail was overturned into a ditch, owing to the fog being so thick that the coachman could not see his horses.

But floods were most to be dreaded. As has been shown, though fogs and snowstorms were great hindrances to locomotion, and the cause of a vast amount of inconvenience and expense, they were seldom attended with loss of life, whereas sad records of fatal issues are to be found in connection with floods, to a few of which I will call the reader's attention.

On September 11th, 1829, when the Birmingham and Liverpool mail reached Smallwood Bridge, it turned out that the bridge had been blown up by the force of the water, and the coachman, not being aware of it, the coach was precipitated into the river.

The guard was washed down under a remaining arch. The coachman caught hold of a stump and saved himself. Of the three inside passengers, one being a slender, active young man, managed to get out by breaking the glass of the window, and helped to save the guard. The two others sunk to the bottom with one of the horses, and nothing could be seen but water.

Strange to say, however, the bags were eventually recovered, when the letters were carefully spread out to dry, and were, most of them, eventually delivered in tolerable condition. Some few fragments are to be seen now at the General Post Office.

Moreton, the guard, was washed down about two hundreds yards, when he caught hold of a tree, and remained there up to his neck in water for an hour before he was rescued.

A most serious flood took place near Newport Pagnel, in November, 1823, though, fortunately, not attended with any fatal consequences, though the stoppage of traffic was very great.

The report to the General Post Office was, "Owing to a sudden rise in the waters near Newport Pagnel, two mails, six coaches, and a van were unable to proceed on their journeys, and, but for the hospitality of Mr. R. Walker, brick-maker, the passengers, amounting to upwards of sixty persons, would have been exposed during the tempestuous night to all the severities of the season. He most kindly opened his doors, and generously offered to the passengers and horses every assistance and comfort in his power ; turning his own horses out of the stables to afford shelter to those of the mails."

On February 9th, 1831, the Milford Haven mail met with a most serious accident.

The following is the report of the inspector, which, though rather involved, affords a graphic account of the circumstances, and I think I cannot do better than give it in his words. He says, " About two o'clock in the morning, when crossing a small bridge near the river Towy, about six miles from Caermarthen, on the London road between Caermarthen and Llandilo, owing to the heavy falls of snow and rain on the mountains and a rapid thaw afterwards, which caused the river to overflow the bridge and high road, the morning also being very dark, and the rain falling heavily, the coach was overtaken by the flood, and before the coachman was aware of it, the water rose to such a height in a few minutes that the four horses were unfortunately drowned, and all on the coach would undoubtedly have shared the same fate but for the meritorious conduct of a passenger named John Cressy (a servant in the employ of Sir Richard Phillips), who swam through the flood for about one hundred yards, and secured some boats, which he brought to their assistance, just as the water had reached the top of the coach, and by this means all the passengers, together with coachman, guard, and mails, were saved. John Cressy was awarded fifteen pounds by the Postmaster-General for his gallant conduct."

Some years after this, but I have not got the date, a somewhat similar accident happened on the down journey of the Gloucester and Aberystwith mail. The water had flooded the road at Lugwardine to a considerable depth, and one of the arches of the bridge had collapsed ; the result of which was that coach, horses, passengers, and all were precipitated into the water, and were with great difficulty rescued, and though no life was lost at the time, one passenger, a Mr. Hardwick, died afterwards from being so long immersed in the water.

CHAPTER V.

NOTHING NEW UNDER THE SUN.

THERE can be but few left now who are able to call to mind that the style of coaches which now run in the summer months from the " White Horse Cellars," and traverse the different roads out of London, were to a great extent anticipated more than fifty years ago. But so it is, and I have a vivid recollection of having seen, in the years 1837 or 38, a remarkably well-appointed coach start from the " Cellars," which created quite a crowd of people, even in those days when coaches were as common as blackberries. It was named the " Taglioni," after a favourite *danseuse* of those days, and ran to Windsor and back in the day. It was painted blue, with a red undercarriage, the family colours of Lord Chesterfield, who horsed it, in conjunction with Count d'Orsay and Prince Bathyani. Young Brackenbury was the professional coachman, for, though his Lordship and his brother proprietors drove very frequently, they kept a curate to do the work when they had other things to do which they liked better. Brackenbury used to wear a most *récherché* blue scarf, with " Taglioni " embroidered on it by the Countess's own hands.

His Lordship had the credit of being a very good coachman, as will be seen from the few lines I venture to produce, which appeared in one of the sporting periodicals of that time :—

> " See Chesterfield advance with steady hand,
> Swish at a rasper and in safety land,
> Who sits his horse so well, or at a race,
> Drives four in hand with greater skill or grace."

No doubt, the " Taglioni " did take her share in the ordinary business of a public conveyance, and not, as in the present day, of carrying only parties on " pleasure bent," but it had a certain spice of the toy about it ; and I should think did not much exercise the minds of Pears or Shepherd, who each had a coach on the same road. As a boy, I had an eye for a coach, and remember, as well as I remember old Keat's birch, seeing those two coaches pass through Eton. Shepherd's was a true blue coach, and travelled on the maxim of " Certain, though slow." Pears drove a coach painted chocolate with red undercarriage, and was altogether a smarter turn-out than the gentle Shepherd, and travelled somewhat faster, but, I believe, ran little chance of being run in for furious driving.

Whilst I stand in fancy upon the classic ground of Eton, there arises before my sight a pageant, which for better or worse has now, like so many other antique customs, passed away never to be revived. I suppose this is a necessary accompaniment of the progress of the age, and that " Montem " could hardly have been carried on in the days of the boiling kettle. It would have been as easy to get blood out of a stone as *salt* from a rushing train ; besides which the present facilities of locomotion would have brought together an exceedingly miscellaneous gathering at Salt Hill, to say the least of it.

Still it was a unique institution, and contained in it a very kindly feeling—that of giving a little start in the world to a youth who had attained the top rung of the college ladder, and was entering upon his university career.

Most of the ways and doings of old Eton have found plenty of chroniclers. The institution in the library is never forgotten. The birch and the block always come in for their fair share of comment, but the triennial festival of " Montem " has, so far as I am aware, not received anything like the same amount of attention ; and as I acted a part in two of them, both in blue and red, I will venture to intrude upon the patience of the reader whilst I make a short digression, emboldened thereto by the fact that Eton customs have already been handled, as well as the ribbons, in a book on coaching.

Well, then, " Montem " was celebrated every third

year. The day's work began by four boys, selected
for the purpose and gaily habited, starting off by
two and two, early in the morning, to scour the principal roads in the neighbourhood, and gather donations
in money—called for the occasion " *Salt*"—from all
the travellers they met with. By this means a nice
sum was collected, which was given to the senior boy
on the foundation upon his leaving the college for the
University of Cambridge. At a later hour, about ten
o'clock, the whole school assembled in the college
square. The sixth form, if I recollect rightly, wore
fancy dresses, representing some classical or historical
characters, and attended by one or two pages, selected
from the lower boys, and also wearing fancy dresses.
The fifth form wore a rather heterogeneous dress, a
mixture of military and civil. It consisted of a red
coat and white trousers, with a sword and sash, sur-
mounted by a cocked hat, from which was fluttering in
the wind a feather, such as was worn by a Field-
Marshal or a General Officer, according to the taste
of the wearer, or in what he could get. The lower
boys were dressed in blue jackets and white trousers,
each carrying in his hand a white wand, in length
about six or seven feet, and in the procession were
mixed alternately with the semi-military fifth form.

In this formation they marched round the quad-
rangle of the college, upon debouching from which a
somewhat strange scene ensued. The wearers of the

red coats drew their swords and began hacking vigorously at the wands, which were held out by their
owners for the purpose of being cut to pieces. The
swords, however, were so blunt that more wands owed
their destruction to the hands of the blue boys than
the swords of the red. The work of destruction being
accomplished, the whole fell in again and marched to
Salt Hill, where dinners were provided for them by
their different houses; and dinner being ended, they
returned to college as they liked.

The two hotels at Salt Hill are, I believe, now
converted to other uses, and the dwellers there would
be as much astonished to see a " Montem," as one of
the hundred and odd mails and coaches which passed
their doors in those days.

CHAPTER VI.

HORSES.

A BOOK about coaching would be very incomplete without touching on the subject of horses, as they were like the main spring of a watch: the coach could not go without them.

Of course, a very large number of horses were employed in the coaches, and I can remember that many people feared that, if coaches ceased to run, the number and quality of the horses bred in the country would deteriorate, in consequence of this demand for them falling off; but that, like most prognostications of the same sort, has proved to be unfounded, and I should think the number of horses at the present time employed in public conveyances, must exceed considerably what it was in the days of road travelling.

However that may be, no doubt very large numbers were kept by the different coach proprietors, both in town and country, at the head of which stood Mr. Chaplin, with about thirteen hundred; and a very large capital was invested in the business, though probably not so large as might be supposed

by the uninitiated; for, judging by my own
experience, I should say that the price of horses
used for that purpose has been over-stated. Nimrod,
who was no doubt a very competent authority on
the subject, at the time he wrote his article in the
Quarterly Review,* puts the average price at twenty-
five pounds, with about thirty pounds for those
working out of London ; but I think those prices are
rather high.

This statement may appear erroneous to those
who would judge by the sums now obtained for the
horses which have been running in the summer
coaches out of London in the present day ; but the
two businesses have little in common, except that the
coaches go on wheels and are drawn by horses. Six
months' work on a coach, loaded as they used to be,
would take more out of the horses employed in them
than would two years in the coaches which look so
pretty at Hatchett's on a fine summer morning, and no
one could have afforded to give high prices for what
wore out so quickly ; not but that horses increased in
value for the work required of them as they became
seasoned to it; but, again, some wore out in the
seasoning. Many horses, doubtless, were bought at
the price of twenty-five pounds, and perhaps in some
cases a little over, though those were exceptional
cases, and for myself, I can say that I never found

* *Quarterly Review* for 1832, vol. 48, pages 346—375.

it necessary to exceed that sum; but in drawing the
average, we must not leave out of the calculation the
large number of horses which found their way into
coaches in consequence of the infirmity of their
tempers, and, I may add, of the bad management they
had been subjected to.

If a horse, though from no fault of his own, ran
away with the parson's or lawyer's "four-wheeler,"
he was immediately offered to the nearest coach
proprietor. If another kicked a commercial traveller
out of his buggy, he was at once offered to the coach
proprietor. If a gentleman's carriage-horse took to
any bad habit, which rendered him unfit for his work,
or unpleasant to the coachman to drive, he also was
offered to the coach proprietor; and I once came into
possession of a very good horse at the price of ten
pounds from this last cause. He had taken to
jibbing, probably because he had a very light mouth,
which caused him to resent the bearing rein, and was
offered to me for the above-named sum, at which I
immediately closed. The coachman brought him to
my stable in time for him to be harnessed and take
his place in the team going out that evening, and he
stayed to witness the start, quite expecting, I make
no doubt, to see some fun. I put him at lead, by the
side of a very good horse, though, by the by, he had
brought a coach to grief when placed alongside of the
pole. Of course, there was no bearing rein, and he

only just stood for a moment till the bars began to rattle against his houghs, when he started off with a bound and a hop, and never gave the slightest trouble.

Horses also got into coaches in consequence of unsoundnesses, which, though little or no detriment to them for work, reduced their market value very considerably; and I once became possessed, for the sum of eighteen pounds, of a very fine horse, nearly thorough-bred, and only five years old, because he had become a roarer, and which had been bought as a hunter for one hundred guineas only a short time previously; but though he ran over a nine-mile stage with some very heavy hills upon it, having no weight on his back, he never made the slightest noise. There are other causes of unsoundness, such as crib-biting, which are no detriment to a coach-horse, though lowering their value in the market.

Then, again, if a horse fell and chipped his knees, whether it arose from any fault or not, he was, as a general rule, sold out of a gentleman's stable; and I once picked up an excellent horse merely for fear he should break his knees. He was a very well-made animal, with the exception that he turned his toes in. He was the property of a clergyman, who must have known little or nothing about horses, and, I suppose, some knowing friend who thought he *did* know must have alarmed him by telling him that the horse was certain to come down with such a pair of forelegs ; so, to save a greater loss, a horse worth thirty pounds at least came into my possession for twenty. So far from falling, he was a safe goer, both in saddle and harness.

The instances to which I have alluded may be classed perhaps more as shortcomings and failings than vice, but to those must be added many whose tempers were apparently incorrigible, and they could only be put in a coach, as those who travelled post would not put up with them.

Just one word *en passant* on that mode of travelling, as it must be quite unknown to the majority of people now living ; but, as one who can recollect it, I venture to say that a well-built comfortable carriage with four post-horses was the perfection of travelling. It is not to be denied that it took a day or two to get over the same distance as is now travelled by a train in a few hours, but the inns on the road were good, generally afforded comfortable accommodation, the cooking was also good, and the wine very fair, of which it was usual to order a bottle for the " good of the house." Some of them had a special character for what were called sleeping-houses, and travellers would continue their journey for an extra stage for the purpose of reaching one of these houses for the night. The attention paid to posting travellers was very great. Upon the carriage stopping at the door, the entrance was perceived to be lined by the hostess, waiters, chambermaids, etc., and the universal question was, " Will you please to alight ? " If they elected to proceed, the cry was immediately raised, " First and second turns out," and in a minute would be seen approaching two mounted postboys, with two other men leading the hand horses, and in about three minutes they were off again, dashing along at about nine miles an hour. If, however, the day's journey was ended, the dusk of evening was exchanged for a comfortable private sitting-room with a bright fire— no public rooms in those days. At the time appointed a comfortable dinner would be served, the *pièce de résistance* being very commonly placed on the table by the host himself. Indeed, one of the great recommendations of the inns of those days was that the host and hostess interested *themselves* in the comfort of their guests. If we add to this the fact that at the beginning of the journey you were taken from your own door, and at the end of it landed at your own or a friend's door, without the experiences of a crowded railway station, there may be something to be said in favour of it.

I can imagine I hear someone say, " Oh, yes, it might have been pleasant enough for those swells who could afford to pay for four horses, but how about the smaller fry who were obliged to be contented with the modest pair ? " Well, I must confess that the odd

mile or two an hour did make a difference, and posting
in a travelling carriage packed with all its boxes, and
containing four or five persons about it, such, in fact,
as was called by the postboys a "*bounder*, having
everything except the kitchen grate," was often,
especially in winter, not unattended with discomfort
and tediousness. How well can I recollect, when
quite a child, at the end of a day's travelling of
seventy or eighty miles on a winter's day, when
twilight was fast sinking into darkness, envying the
people who I could see through the windows of the
houses, sitting round a blazing fire ! And, indeed, the
blacksmith, blowing up the fire on his hearth and
making the sparks fly from the iron by the blows
administered by his brawny arms, possessed much
attraction. This, however, was quite made up for on
the down journey later in the year. This, indeed, was
unalloyed delight. After having been "cribbed,
cabined, and confined" in London for five months,
with nothing more nearly approaching to the country
than Hyde Park and Kensington Gardens (and in
those days there was not a flower-bed in either of
them), when one emerged from the suburbs, which
was sooner done in those days than now, and the eye
beheld the fields and green hedges, made brilliant by
wild flowers, it seemed a very Elysium ; and to hold
in one's hand a posy of dog-roses was bliss itself,
even though they had received a peppering of road

dust. I have always loved a dog-rose since, and shall continue to do so as long as I live. The longest summer day was hardly long enough for taking in such happiness. No amount of railway travelling will ever leave behind such happy reminiscences of childhood. Then, again, there was time and opportunity for other things, which can never be the case in railway travelling; amongst which was the childish pleasure of being fitted with a new straw hat whilst the horses were being changed at Dunstable. It was not all *couleur de rose*, neither was it all labour and sorrow. Like all other things in this world, it had its lights and shades.

Perhaps it may be urged against this that there is no time for such a mode of travelling now. It may be so, but, as a nearly worn-out old roadster, it strikes me there may be too much haste for comfort. It was undeniably slow and expensive, though it may be doubted whether people generally spent more money in travelling than they do now. The facilities offered by railways cause the present generation to move about a great deal more freely than did their ancestors.

But all this is skirting, and I must return to the scent, which was, I think, very much the sort of horses which we coachmen had to drive. They were, indeed, often a very queer lot, but they had to be driven, and were driven. Of course, four of this sort

were not put all together; there were always one or
two steady ones among them.   But even if they had
been, and all had determined to do wrong, it is most
improbable that all would have gone wrong in the
same way, and one could have been played off against
another.   This is one great advantage in four.   In
single harness, if the horse takes to bad ways, you have
the whole team against you, but that is, as I have said,
very unlikely with four.   Perhaps this may account
for the old saying that "half the coachmen were killed
out of gigs."

When I got a horse that was very troublesome, I
always found that doubling him, that is, making him
run his stage double, brought him to his senses in the
course of a week or two.   Some may say it was not
right to risk the lives and limbs of the passengers, by
using unruly horses, but, practically, very little danger
was incurred.   I will not say that no accidents ever
occurred from this cause, but they were very rare.   If
an accident should have happened, and a life been
lost from that cause, the old law of " deodand " would
have touched up the proprietor's pockets severely ;
besides which, horses of this description were only
entrusted to the hands of well-tried men.

Notwithstanding all this, however, accidents did
occasionally happen from this cause, and sometimes of a
very serious nature, one or two of which I will now produce.   The first was an exceedingly calamitous one, and

I think I cannot do better than use the words of a friend of mine, who was an eye-witness to the scene, as they will be more likely to convey a full idea of the horrible appearance presented by the mingled heap of injured human beings and horses, with the coach on the top of them, than anything I can say at second hand. He says: " I was staying at the 'White Horse,' at Hockliffe, for a few days, and on the first night I was disturbed by a man knocking at the front door and shouting, 'Get up, the " Greyhound " is overturned and all the passengers are killed.' Upon hearing of this terrific slaughter," he proceeds to say, " I got up, and with others started to the scene of the catastrophe, which was about a mile and a half distant, opposite to a large mansion called 'Battleden House,' then the residence of Sir G. P. Turner, and there we found a mass of human beings and horses all of a heap. The coachman was under the coach with his leg broken, many of the passengers dangerously injured, and two horses had legs broken. It was a shocking sight to witness, and melancholy to hear the squealing of horses, and the passengers moaning."

After all, however, it was found that there was not so much damage done here to the passengers as would have been expected. None were killed, nor any so seriously injured but that they were able to be conveyed to their destinations in a few days.

The cause of the accident originated in the near

side wheeler accomplishing what she had tried
to do many times before, viz., kick over the pole,
which broke, when, of course, all control was lost,
and the coach was overturned into the ravine where it
was found.

In the other case no injury was sustained by anyone except the culprit himself, who must have been
an exceedingly violent brute.

In October, 1839, when near Maidenhead a horse
in the Bristol mail kicked so violently that he broke
the pole-hook and harness, and put out his own
shoulder in his fall.

Blind horses, again, found their way into coaches,
and, if high mettled ones, performed very good work.
The worst of them was, that they became too
knowing about the corners, and when at wheel, where
they were generally driven (though in Ireland I have
had both leaders blind), if the coachman was not on
the look out for it, might hang him into one. Some
however, were very bold, and high couraged. I
recollect one which ran in the lead of the "Greyhound" out of Shrewsbury, of this sort. He was so
handsome a horse, that, if he had been all right, he
would have commanded at least a hundred guineas for
a gentleman's carriage, but being blind, of course, was
only fit for a coach. One day, when I was travelling
by that coach, and was as usual driving, he quite
won my heart by the high couraged manner in which

he elbowed his way through the large droves of cattle which were being driven along the road from Shrewsbury fair.

The reader will now understand how it came to pass that the average value of coach-horses was so low, as these blemished, unsound, and vicious ones never cost more than fifteen pounds, and very often not much above half that sum. I once purchased a good mare for the very modest figure of twenty-five shillings. It may be asked, how was it possible to buy a horse fit to run a coach, or indeed do any fast work, for such a sum? to which I reply, that she had only one place where she could possibly be utilized, and that at the time she came into my possession coaches were continually being supplanted by railways, and therefore there was very little demand for such as her. She had neither size nor form for a wheeler, even if she would have condescended to go there, and only of use on one side at lead, I forget which, and I suppose would very promptly have made fragments of any carriage behind her in single harness. She was, however, a real good leader where she chose to go, and I drove her in a match team of chestnuts for a considerable time. I bought her with confidence, as I had frequently driven her in another coach previously.

Talking of only going on one side, I do not think coachmen always consider this enough. There is a theory with many gentlemen, and their coachmen, that the sides should be changed frequently; but with hard work, such as that in a coach, horses do their work better and easier to themselves by always going in the same place. At one time I was horsing a coach, and driving one side, as it was called, another coachman driving the other; and, consequently, we both drove the same horses over some stages. He said to me, "That in one of my teams, one leader could not go up to the other." I asked him on which side he drove him. He replied, "I put him on the off side, because I can get at him better there." I said, "You try the near side," which was where I always drove him, "and you will not want to get at him." Of course, if a horse begins to hang to one side, it has become time to change him.

The vices which most commonly brought horses into coaches were jibbing and kicking. I do not recollect to have ever known a case of either of them being thoroughly eradicated, though they were sufficiently kept under to render them of little moment; but they were liable to return if a fresh hand took hold of them, especially if he showed any signs of indecision. It is astonishing how soon horses find out a change of hand.

The great thing to attend to with jibbers is not to keep them standing. If they have time to plant themselves they will give trouble; but if the coachman is up and off at once, they will generally start.

With kickers at wheel I never found two or three good punishments over the ears to fail in bringing them into subjection, or, at any rate, sufficiently so, though a "ventilated" front boot might occasionally be the result. With a road coach, however, this did not much signify. A leader might be harder to tame, as he cannot be got at in the same way. I have heard it said of some one that he was so excellent a whip that he could hit a fly on a leader's ear. I can only say I never saw it done. But if a leader will not stand still to kick, he can be driven; kick and keep going doesn't much matter.

In justice to the horses, however, it must be said that they are not the only ones to blame. No small number of them are rendered vicious, or unsteady, by mismanagement, and irremediable mischief is not unfrequently produced from quite unexpected causes. To give one instance: I am convinced that many a leader is set kicking by the pole-chains being too slack.

I fancy I hear someone say, "What on earth have the pole-chains to do with the leaders?" Well, I will try and show how intimately they are connected.

When pulling up or going down-hill, the wheel horses must come back towards the coach sufficiently to tighten the pole-chains. They will thus be nearer the coach, or further off, by just that number of inches. Then, as the leaders' reins are held in the same place as the wheelers', they must also come back by the same number of inches, which may, in the case of very slack pole-chains, be sufficient to allow the bars to fall upon the leaders' houghs, which is a fertile source of kicking; and it is a very true saying that a horse which has once kicked in harness is never to be trusted again.

For a large number of jibbers I believe the bearing rein to be responsible. But, after all, horses are queer creatures. They have as many fads and fancies as men and women. Some will kick for being touched in one spot, and some in another. I drove a leader for some time who was easily set kicking by the bar touching him above his houghs; but upon lengthening his traces by two or three holes, so as to let the bar fall below the hough, in case it should touch him, he was quite contented. And, again, some horses will kick when touched by a low pole, others by a high one.

Coupling reins also are frequently so arranged as to be a cause of discomfort to horses. It is manifest that when one horse carries his head high, and his partner low, the coupling rein of the former should be above that of the latter; and, again, if one horse tosses his head, and his coupling rein is the under one, he must cause much annoyance to the other, especially if he has a light mouth.

Parliament has now passed a Bill for the purpose of regulating the traffic in horseflesh. Such an Act, if it had been placed on the Statute Book, and had resulted in creating a demand for horseflesh for food, would have been a great boon to stage coachmen formerly, as they would not have been called upon to wear out the old horses. It would have paid the proprietors better to put them up to feed when they became stale, and fatten them for the market. It would also have prevented much suffering to horses.

And now, if any reader is astonished at the price of horses, if he has never heard of a less price for a set of harness than sixty guineas, he will be incredulous when I mention the cost of that generally used with coaches. Eighteen pounds was the top price usually given, and I have driven with well-shaped and good-looking harness which only cost sixteen. Indeed, at Walsall, which was the chief emporium for low-priced harness, if two or three sets were taken at the same time, they could be had for eleven pounds each. Collars were not included.

Of course, such harness as this did not last long, and, perhaps, was not the cheapest in the long run; though I doubt whether the leather was not better then than it is now, being all tanned with oak bark.

CHAPTER VII.

THE ROADS.

As the railways are dependent upon the excellence of
the permanent way for the pace at which they can
travel, so were coaches indebted to the good state of
the roads for the great speed at which they were able
to perform their journeys by day and night ; and it
may be safely said, without fear of contradiction, that
in no other country had they been brought so near to
perfection, although a good deal of improvement still
remained to be done, and would have been effected
if the railway era had been postponed for another
decade. Everything that could be thought of to
lighten the draught was being adopted. Not only
were hills cut down and valleys filled up, but on one
hill on the Holyhead road, between Dunstable and
Brickhill, a tram of granite had been laid on one
side of the road to render the draught lighter to
carriages ascending the hill, though it had been very
greatly eased by a deep cutting through the chalk. I
was one day travelling up by the "Wonder," and
when going up this hill, Harry Liley, who was driving,

although it was a hard frost, put the wheels upon the tram to show me what a help it was to the horses. If it was of so much benefit when the frost had hardened the road, what must it have been when the road was soft ? If these trams had become general, they would have saved the extra pair of horses which used to be frequently employed to pull the fast coaches up the worst ascents. Notwithstanding all that had been done on the main roads, there remained miles and miles of cross roads which were traversed by coaches at high speed, where little had been effected in the way of lowering hills, and it was then that the greatest care and skill were required to ensure the safety of heavily loaded coaches.

It must be recollected that up to quite the latter end of the great coaching days no patent breaks were in use. They were not invented till about the year 1835, and were very slow in coming into use. I knew a case of the Post Office authorities refusing their sanction for the proprietors to have one attached to a mail coach at their own expense, because they thought it would break the contract with the coachmaker, and I can quite imagine that the breaks were no favourites of those who miled the coaches, as there was not only the original cost, but the use of one has a considerable influence in wearing out the hind wheels.

I had on one occasion undertaken to horse a coach over a stage, when the coach was supplied by

7

one of the proprietors, and to save his hind wheels he wanted to omit the break. I immediately said, that no horse of mine would be put to a coach which was sent out without a break, as I believed them to be a great security against accidents. I have known of one instance, however, where a break caused an accident instead of preventing it, but then the hind wheels must have been in a shameful condition, as they both broke upon its application.

I really think that wheel horses held back better in the days before breaks came into use than they do now. It was then necessary to take a hill in time, as it was called, which meant going slowly over the brow, and about half-way down it ; and horses were, by this means, better educated in holding than they are now, when it is not generally necessary even to slacken the pace at all, as the pressure upon the horses can be regulated by the break. This is also an enormous help to a fast coach, even if it did not render the use of the skid almost unnecessary.

I was once talking this subject over with little Bob Leek, who, from having driven the " Hirondelle " for some years, was a very competent judge, and I remarked that I thought a break was worth a mile an hour to a coach. He replied, he thought it was worth two, and I have little doubt he was right over hilly roads, such as some which the " Hirondelle " travelled over.

It was to the system of turnpike trusts, now unfortunately no more, that this country is indebted for the general excellence of its roads, and against which I never heard more than two objections raised. One, that it was very unpleasant and annoying to be obliged to stop at the toll bars and pull out the money when the fingers were cold, and the other, that it was a very expensive method of collecting money. The first of these objections, I think, may be passed over in silence. It, no doubt, is unpleasant to do anything which requires the use of the fingers when they are cold, but surely that should not be held to be sufficient reason for putting an end to a system which in the main worked well. To the second a plea of guilty must be returned ; but with mitigating circumstances. Indeed, there was no necessity for it at all, if the trustees had carried out their work well.

The " pikers," as they were called, did, no doubt, make a good living out of the business, but so do most middlemen, and they need not have been permitted to make an exorbitant profit. But before going further, perhaps, I had better explain what a "piker" is, as they, like the dodo, no longer exist. Well, then, they were a class of men who leased the turnpike tolls, each of them generally taking all the gates in a larger or smaller district. Sam Weller said they were " Misanthropes who levied tolls on mankind ; " but, as a general rule, these men did not collect themselves, but employed others to do it, who resided in the houses. Of course, these "pikers," like other people, thought their first duty was to themselves, and they usually put their heads together previous to the lettings of the gates, and agreed to divide the spoils amicably, instead of bidding against one another. There was nothing, however, to prevent the trustees putting in collectors, the same as the pikers did, and by that means find out the real value of the tolls, and at the same time keep Mr. Piker up to the scratch. This, indeed, was often done, but when it was omitted, great losses were incurred, as I have found to my own advantage.

The tolls were not levied under the General Turnpike Act of Parliament, but under local Acts, and it was usual to insert in these local Acts a clause compelling coaches to pay toll both going and returning, even if drawn by the same horses. This, I think, was a decided hardship, but it was generally mitigated by the pikers allowing them to pay for only three horses instead of four, making six a day instead of eight, and this led to a contest which I once had with a piker.

At the first gate, a short distance out of Machynlleth, the lessee of it refused this concession to the "Harkaway" coach; therefore, when the day arrived for the annual letting, my partner and myself outbid him and took the gate, putting in a collector, and at the end of the year, after paying for the collecting, we had fifty pounds to divide between us. Now, I think I have shown that if proper care was taken by the trustees, no necessity existed, on this score, for abandoning the turnpike system, for in this one example they gratuitously threw away at least sixty pounds a year, which ought to have been available for repairing the roads.

In another trust on the same road, the trustees tried to be a little too sharp. As I have already said, the tolls were levied under local Acts, and in this case, the special clause relating to coaches had been, either intentionally or inadvertently, omitted, and we consequently claimed that the coach should, like all other conveyances, be exempted from paying if returning with the same horses. The trustees, however, contended that a public conveyance was liable to pay both ways, independently of a special clause to that effect. The question was referred to counsel's opinion, which was given in favour of the coach, and this so exasperated the trustees that they proceeded in hot haste to erect a new toll-gate to catch it after the change of horses.

In their hurry, however, they forgot that there were yet three months before the annual letting of the gates, and they found themselves face to face with the difficulty that no one could be persuaded to become a lessee for that short period.

In this dilemma, we coach proprietors stepped in, and, *faute de mieux*, were accepted as lessees, the result being that, instead of paying the toll at the end of the three months, we retired from the business with a profit of thirty shillings, after paying the expenses of collecting.

On the day following, the stables were changed to the other side of the gate, and the coach ran through free with a ticket from the previous one.

These seem small things to write about, but they afforded some interest and amusement at the time, and may be worth mentioning as being a sample of the life.

The turnpike system, no doubt, like all other human inventions, had its defects, but to it we are indebted for the excellence of our internal communications ; and I cannot help thinking that it was unjust both to the bondholders and the ratepayers to allow it to die out. Though the former were fairly liable to the diminished value of their property caused by the rivalry of the railways, they, or those before them, had honestly lent their money upon the understanding that the Acts of Parliament would be renewed from time to time, and it was little short of robbery to allow them to expire. Hardships, no doubt, did exist in some districts from the excessive number of the toll gates, especially in Wales, where it was no uncommon thing to be called upon to pay at three gates in a distance of ten or twelve miles.

This was found so burdensome that it produced the Rebecca riots in South Wales, which led to the passing of an excellent Act for that part of the Principality, and if that Act had been extended to North Wales and England, the turnpike gates would, most probably, have been standing at the present day, and I know not who would have been losers by it, except the doctors and the timber merchants and other hauliers. At any rate, the cost of repairing the roads fell on those who enjoyed the benefit. The system, on the whole, worked well, and might easily have been made to work better, and I entertain no doubt, indeed, I know it, that large numbers of those who clamoured against it, would now recall it if possible. If it was expensive to collect the tolls, it appears to be impossible to collect a wheel and van tax.

It is easier to destroy than to build up, and I only hope that, after the same length of trial, it may not be found that it would have been wiser if we had remained contented with the old form of county government, which had done its work so well for a great number of years.

Since the above was penned the South Wales Turnpike Act has expired, thereby saddling £25,000 a year upon those who do not use the roads, instead of upon those who do. Where is Rebecca now?

CHAPTER VIII.

A SCIENTIFIC CHAPTER.

I HAD intended to conclude my remarks on the subject of the mail coaches, but have been induced to invest in another chapter by an ingenious proposal which was brought to the notice of the Postmaster-General in the year 1807. If it led to no results, at any rate it shows that there were those who took a keen interest in the subject.

The Rev. W. Milton, Rector of Heckfield, Hartford Bridge—the same reverend gentleman whose acquaintance we have previously made as the advocate of broad wheels—invented a coach, which he claimed would prevent overturns and breakdowns. The body of it was this shape, which I give as it appears in the minutes on the subject, still preserved at the General Post-Office. It is certainly singularly deficient in graceful curves, and I can only suppose that it

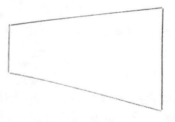

is meant to indicate the manner in which the luggage box was placed. At any rate, we are told that the coach was so constructed that nearly all the luggage was carried in a box below the body of the carriage, which was not higher than usual; but the appearance of the coach was deemed heavy, and as the load was low, it was thought that the draught would be heavier than the coaches then in use. Many coaches which loaded heavily with luggage were already furnished with a receptacle for it denominated the "slide," which was fixed under the hind axle, and thus, no doubt, did add considerably to the draught; but to remedy this, as we shall see, Mr. Milton makes use of unusually high wheels.

To prevent breakdowns the coach was fitted with idle wheels on each side of the luggage box, with their periphery below the floor, and each as near as was requisite to its respective active wheel. These idle wheels were ready, in case of breakdowns on either side, to catch the falling carriage, and instantly to continue its previous velocity, till the coachman could pull up the horses. The bottom of the luggage box was fourteen inches from the ground, and the idle wheel five or six inches. The following extracts will convey a better idea of the value of the invention. It evidently received a practical trial:—

"Mr. Ward, the coachman, soon found what he might venture, and he took the coach accordingly

over such ground as would most assuredly have
caused an overturn of any stage-coach with its usual
load. This was repeatedly done in the presence of
six insides and ten outsides, besides the coachman.
Seven parts, perhaps, in ten of the load, which was
nearly three tons, lay on the hind wheels. These, by
the patentee's directions, were six feet high, and with
no dishing, and, as he deemed, sufficiently strong.
They did not fail; but it was the opinion of Mr.
Thomas Ward, and all the practical men on the spot,
that they were not such as could show the principle
of safety as to dangerous and side-long ground up to
its full extent. As it was, however, any common
coach would have gone over at fifty different places
during the stage which this coach took without the
least symptom of overturning. A linch-pin of one of
the hind wheels was taken out. The coach went on,
and presently off came the wheel, and down dropped
the carriage about seven inches on a small idle wheel,
which immediately continued the motion without the
least inconvenience to the outside passengers or
puzzle to the horses, and the shock was not greater
than what was produced by taking over a stone in
the night, and, if it had been required, the coach
might have been taken five or six miles by means of
the idle wheel; and Mr. Thomas Ward very con-
fidently thinks these two circumstances of safety would
invariably attend any stage-coach so constructed."

So confident was the reverend patentee that he
wrote the following challenge : " I have no fear that
either science or practice can effectually controvert
the following remark : Supposing, in a stage-coach
as at present, that the centre of gravity be four feet
above the main axle, and the width on the ground
the same in two cases, then the higher the wheels
the greater will be the danger of an overturn from
an equal cause. It is not so with me, for the higher
the wheels the deeper may the luggage box be, so
that the antidote follows the growth of the danger ;
and here, from the full conviction I have of its truth,
I wish to offer the following opinion : Let seven or
eight parts in ten of the total load be within the hind
wheels, and let them be at least six feet high, on
horizontal cylindric arms, by this disposition, compared
against the present, more than one horse in forty
would be saved or spared, for the goodness of the
draught would come out even through the intricacy
of the medium, the fore-carriage ; but in many coaches
the door at the middle of the side does not permit so
advantageous a hind wheel, and that at the expense
just mentioned."

The invention was not accepted by the Postmaster-
General, although it was, to some extent, admitted to
combine a principle of safety with the celerity required
in mail carriages. The cost, however, of such a
change in the mail coaches would have been very

heavy, which, no doubt, had a good deal to do with its rejection.

The fact, however, is that these inventions were not wanted, clever as they might have been and effective where required. The mail coaches were not called upon to travel over " dangerous and side-long ground," but upon fairly good roads at the worst, for which the coaches, as then constructed, possessed quite sufficient stability, and the idle wheels, however great the security they would have imparted to heavily-loaded stage-coaches, were not required on the mails, where the sustaining power was so great in proportion to the comparatively light loads which they carried, that a broken axle was unknown among them, and it was impossible for a wheel to come off with Mr. Vidler's axle and boxes; and, of course, the idle wheels must have added to the weight.

Although these patent-safety coaches were rejected by the Post-office, they did find favour in one or two quarters. One worked for some time between London and Stroudwater, and several were in use in Reading, as the following certificate will prove :—

" We, the proprietors of the Reading coaches, beg leave thus jointly to inform our friends and the public that we have each of us, during the last five weeks, tried the Rev. W. Milton's patent-safety coach, built by Brown and Day. We are fully persuaded that its draught will be as fair as that of any coach on the road, and have such a conviction of the safety of its principles, that we have no doubt that we shall be induced to put them on as early as shall be convenient to every coach we have.

"Signed,

"WILLIAMS & Co., Coachmasters, London and Reading;

"E. EDWARDS, Coachmaster, Reading;

"J. MOODY, Coachmaster, London."

It is very disappointing that no drawing appears to have been preserved showing what these coaches looked like when they stood up upon their wheels; but evidently the patent parts were capable of being applied to the ordinary coaches, as is proved by the following portion of an advertisement :—

"Any particulars regarding these coaches and the application of the principles of it to stage-coaches at present in use may be had by applying to Brown and Day, Coachmakers, Reading." And again they say, "The safety of the plan depends upon the union of the two principles. The same charge will be made for the application of the luggage box or idle wheels, where either may be required separately, as for the two together."

The Postmaster-General appears to have been fortunate in the number of his counsellors, but, judging by the following suggestion, it would have required a very great multitude to produce wisdom.

Indeed, a more objectionable change could hardly have been thought of.

By a memorandum at the General Post-Office, it appears that in February, 1831, the Rev. W. C. Fenton, of Doncaster, made a suggestion that postilions should be substituted for the coachmen. The suggestion was rejected, as it was considered that the change of postilions would necessarily be much more frequent than the change of coachmen, and therefore the chances of delays would be greatly multiplied. It was also thought that, were such a mode of driving adopted, it would be the means of raising the fares, and the mails would again require support. Many of the coachmen drove from forty to fifty miles without a change. The Postmaster-General, Duke of Richmond, considered the horses had enough to do without carrying additional weight.

The horses would not only have had the weight of an extra man to share among them, but they would have had to carry both men in a way best calculated to distress them. The easiest way for a horse to move a weight is by his draught, the worst when placed upon his back.

Then again there was the difficulty of who was to pay the postilions. They must have been changed at every stage, and I should think the passengers, although in those days pretty well accustomed to giving fees of one sort or another, would have objected to being *kicked* by two postboys at the end of every stage.

I can fancy I hear one of the uninitiated exclaim, " I should think they would object to such treatment as that at any time," but, in the language of the road, the word *kicking* had no brutal signification attached to it—it only meant asking the passengers for their fees, and the word *shelling* was often used to express the same process in less objectionable language. The word was understood something in the way that an Irishman uses the word *kilt*, which the following anecdote will explain :—

An English gentleman had rented some shooting in Ireland, and had gone over to enjoy the sport. On the morning after his arrival, having engaged a lot of boys to beat for him, he started off to look for game, but before he had gone very far, after firing a shot, he heard a great commotion and chatter among the boys. Thereupon he called out to them to ask if anything was the matter, to which the answer he received was, " Nothing your 'anour,' only you've kilt a boy." I need hardly say, that, being a stranger to the country, he was very much alarmed till he reached the spot where the boys were assembled, when he discovered, to his infinite relief, that the word " kilt " conveyed no mortal signification in that country.

I will venture to give a few more instances of the

propositions made to the Postmaster-General. Some were certainly ingenious, but he very wisely could not be induced to give up a system which had been well proved, for what at the best, and however clever in itself, was untried.

On September 14th, 1816, Mr. Peter M'Kenzie of Paddington offered to construct a steam engine to run on rails at the rate of fifteen miles an hour. He asserted that the mountains of Wales or any other part of the United Kingdom would not impede its velocity. To enable him to build a small model he asked that a hundred and fifty or two hundred pounds might be advanced to him. As may be supposed this was refused him, and the plan was abandoned. This gentleman also claimed that in 1802 the idea of printing newspapers by steam first originated with him.

Mr. John England, writing from Aberdeen in August, 1820, wants the department to adopt a travelling carriage or machine, which was impelled by means of the expansion and contraction of compound fluids. The machine was stated to weigh about 90 lbs. The plan was not entertained. Again, in the year 1832 the same person submitted an improved machine worked on the same principle, but, as may be imagined, it met with no better result than the first.

In the next suggestion we appear to be approaching the present railway system, but I should suppose that he intended laying his rails by the side of the turnpike roads.

Mr. Thomas Gray, writing from Brussels in November, 1821, suggests steam coaches on iron rails. In support of it, he stated that the journey to Edinburgh would be done in half the time taken by the mail coaches, and that the expense of laying the iron rails would be more than covered by the extra passengers that could be carried in the additional coaches which could be run.

This also met with a cold reception, and no doubt appeared at the time to be simply speculative, yet the light of time compels us to take a different view, and to recognize in it the germs of a great invention.

Mr. James Rondeen, of Lambeth, on June 3rd, 1823, submitted a scheme to convey the mails by engines consuming their own smoke, of four or six-horse power, which would cost from two hundred and fifty to three hundred pounds each, and impel a coach at the rate of from fifteen to twenty miles an hour. He estimated that there were two hundred and eighty coaches running daily from London and on the cross roads, the work of which, if his scheme was adopted, would be performed by eighty-two engines. This scheme was considered an extraordinary one, but the condition of its acceptance imposed by the inventor could not be complied with.

8

I should gather from what is said here, that Mr.
Rondeen's plan was of the nature of a traction engine
to run upon the existing turnpike roads, and, if I am
right, the Postmaster-General of that day had a better
opinion of that mode of progression than of the
system of rails. No doubt, several descriptions of
traction engines were tried, but none succeeded, and
I have heard of surveyors of turnpike roads laying
such extra thick coverings of stone on the roads as to
clog the engine wheels; but however this may be,
experience has proved that they are not capable of
much pace, however useful they may be found for
slow traffic.

A Mr. Knight, in January, 1822, suggested an
elevated road or railway. The carriage was to be
slung from the road on rails above, and two men,
suspended in it at the bottom, would turn machinery
to propel it along the groove or railway. After the
idea had been talked over by Mr. Knight with the
head of the mail coach department, the latter was
satisfied that it would be of no use to the Post-office.

A Mr. Elmes of Regent Street, in October, 1823,
offered to convey the mails to any part of the United
Kingdom at the rate of from fifteen to seventeen
miles an hour, by means of a mechanical carriage,
which could be worked by horses or not. He stated
that his contrivance would reduce the cost of
conveyance to about a quarter of that then incurred.

It need hardly be said that this proposal was too indefinite to be entertained.

On the 25th of November, 1826, a Mr. Thorold, of Great Milton, Norfolk, suggested the application of steam to mail coaches for propelling them on turnpike roads. This plan appears to have been considered feasible, as it is recorded that the plan was not adopted, as it was considered best to wait until the idea was *seen* in practice.

On April 27, 1826, a Mr. Cadogan Williams submitted a plan for the rapid conveyance of mails by means of tubes. The outline of his plan was this : That a square of cast-iron or brick be laid from one stage to another, with its extremities communicating with vaults of sufficient magnitude for the purpose ; one vault having an air-evaporating apparatus, and the other a condensing, such as is used to blow iron furnaces worked by steam power. At the neck of the tube joining the condensing apparatus should be two stoppers, on the principle of those that are used in beer cocks. Between the stoppers should be a door for putting in the box of letters. On closing it the stoppers should be turned, and the condensed air would exert itself in the box and produce its rapid movement. This was certainly very ingenious, if somewhat complicated. At any rate, he was informed that his plan was not applicable to the purposes of the department.

And now comes a really wonderful proposal. A Mr. Slade, on May 14, 1827, offered to convey the mails at the rate of a mile a minute; but he appears not to have been of a very communicative disposition, as he did not state by what means this very high rate of speed was to be obtained, but he estimated the cost for carrying out his plan at two thousand pounds a mile. As may be supposed, this was considered too visionary and costly to be enquired into further.

And now I have got what I think will raise a smile. It will hardly be believed, but so it was, that a Royal Engineer—an officer, I suppose—suggested that the mails should be conveyed by means of shells and cannon. His idea was to enclose the letters in shells and then fire them to the next stage, three miles distant, and then to the next stage, and so on to the end of the journey. He said a good bombardier could drop the shell within a few feet of the spot where the next one was stationed.

As early as the year 1811 a trial was made of a drag, or break, apparently a good deal resembling the breaks now so generally applied to wheels. In that year a drag, as it was then called, was introduced by a Mr. Simpson to the Post-office authorities, and was tried on the Brighton and Worcester mails; but the advantages claimed for it by the patentee were not borne out in practice. The advantages claimed were that in case of the reins or pole breaking, or horses running away, the drag could be at once applied by the guard without leaving his seat, as it was put in action by a lever or shaft affixed to the body of the coach, and worked by hand. It does not appear, however, to have possessed sufficient attractions for it to be brought into general use, as nothing more is heard of it. In the year 1811 I don't suppose there was much to be feared from horses running away!

Before quite taking leave of science I will venture to touch upon a subject which, if not exactly science, is nearly related to it. At any rate, it can only be solved, if at all, through the medium of science. I can fancy I hear some votary of science exclaim with some indignation, "What is this doughty question which is to puzzle science?" To this I can only answer that if science has or can solve it satisfactorily, I humbly beg its pardon for doubting its powers. Well, the subject I am raising is expressed by the word *Traction*. Traction, I mean, as connected with pace. What is the difference in power required to move a given load at ten miles an hour and at five miles an hour? I have somewhere seen it argued as if it was the same, and that therefore the horses must suffer greatly over the latter part of a stage, supposing that their powers were less and the weight to be drawn remained the same. Of course, the weight does in one sense continue the same, but every

coachman who has had any experience in driving will
have observed how much longer time it requires to
pull up a coach going at a high speed than one at a
slow pace; which of itself proves that after the
coach is once set in motion and has acquired a fast
pace, the exertion required to keep it going is
considerably reduced. Without for a moment
forgetting the cardinal truth that " it is the pace which
kills," it is quite apparent that the disease and the
remedy, to some extent at least, travel together.
Another fact which can be attested by all old stage
coachmen, and which goes strongly to prove how
much reduced the draught is by pace, is that four
light horses can get a load up a steep pitch at a gallop
which they would be quite incapable of surmounting
at a walk.

Then there is another item which adds to the
complexity, which is this—that the greater the weight,
the longer the time required for pulling up. It would
seem, therefore, as if a heavy weight, to a certain
extent, assisted its own propulsion. The same
circumstances are observed on the railways, and,
probably, from the hardness of the metal on which
their wheels run, it is still more apparent than on a
road. I was once travelling for a short distance upon
a locomotive engine without a train behind it, and
upon asking the driver how long it would take to
bring his engine to a standstill, he said, " I could stop

it almost immediately now, but it would be very different with a long train behind her." Probably there are few coachmen who have driven any great number of miles through whose brain this question has never trotted, but without arriving at any solution of it. At any rate, I confess my own ignorance, and only throw down the question at the feet of science after the custom of the ages of chivalry, when the herald threw down the gauntlet into the midst of the assembled knights, to be picked up by the best man.

The following narrative will convey some idea of the force of velocity which appertains to the wheels of a coach travelling at a high speed :—

As the "Mazeppa" coach was proceeding on her journey from Monmouth to Gloucester, when descending a hill about three miles from the former place at a fast pace, the tire of the near hind wheel came off, and the impetus was so great that it caused it to pass the coach and run on for nearly half a mile, thus proving that the power required to draw a carriage when it has attained much speed must be very much diminished. It only requires to be kept moving.

CHAPTER IX.

A NOTE ON THE HORN.

MANY guards on the day coaches carried key bugles, on which some of them were able to play exceedingly well, and helped to while away many a half hour on the journey ; but on the mails and night coaches, the former especially, straight horns were employed. Formerly these were all made of tin, hence the "yard of tin," but in later years a good many copper or brass ones came into use, and a few, in quite late years, adopted a twisted horn without keys, much like the infantry field bugle used in the army.

These horns, of whichever sort, were generally efficacious in warning carts, carriages, or other vehicles to get out of the way, but were of little avail against the worst obstruction met with on the roads. At that time all the sheep, cattle and pigs which travelled from one part of the country to another were obliged to make use of the highways, and though the drovers were possessed of marvellous skill in avoiding the turnpike roads on account of the tolls, nevertheless large droves and flocks were not unfrequently met with,

J.Sturgess del. et lith.

OBSTRUCTION ON THE BRIDGE.

M&N Hanhart imp.

and were the cause of considerable delay, and also sometimes of altercation. I was once forcing my way through a large drove of cattle, rather more unceremoniously than the drover approved of, when he threw his heavy stick at my head, and only narrowly missed it ; and here perhaps it will not be out of place to introduce a few cases which exhibit the danger incurred by coaches from the presence of cattle and sheep, whether in droves and flocks or straying on the roads.

On November 7th, 1789, the Preston and Carlisle mail, after changing horses at Garstang, when about three miles on the road to Preston, in crossing a bridge over the Lancaster and Preston canal, encountered some drove cattle in the road, when the coach was coming down the bridge, which is a declivity, and the coachman pulled his horses too much to the off-side of the road to avoid the cattle, and the off wheels ran up the bank and upset the coach. Nobody seems to have been injured.

A curious accident happened to the Devonport mail *en route* to Bath, on November 7th, 1839. The guard's report says : "A short distance from New House, a bullock straying on the road became frightened at the light of the lamps, and attempted to leap the hedge, but falling back against the leaders, the horses all sprung across the road, and running the coach into the hedge, threw the coach-

man off the box, and the wheels passed over him."
He, the guard, then proceeds to say that he
only lost one hour and a half's time, but gives no
account of what became of the coachman. His
whole thoughts appear to have been concentrated on
his business, and he reminds one of the anecdote
about the trainer and the old woman.

As a string of race-horses were out at exercise
one morning, one of them bolted and came into
collision with some obstacle which threw him down,
seriously injuring him, and killing the lad who was
riding him. The unfortunate lad was soon removed,
and the trainer was lamenting over the horse when he
was accosted by an old woman, who happened to be
passing by at the time, and began to condole with him
on the accident. He replied, "Ah! it is a bad job,
indeed, I am afraid he will never be able to run for
another race ;" but, says she, " How's the poor boy ? "
" Oh ! drat the boy, he's dead," was the answer.

Sheep were sometimes the cause of accidents. On
January 10th, 1840, when the London and Hull
mail was within a mile of Peterborough, the horses
shied at a flock of sheep, and ran the coach into a
ditch six feet deep, overturning it, and causing three
hours' loss of time.

And now, having indulged in a stave on the guards'
horns, perhaps the coachmen's whips may feel themselves neglected if I have no word to say about them,

and on this subject it must be admitted that rather different opinions prevailed. *Tot homines tot sententiæ.* Some preferred, I think most professionals did, a stiff crop and a light thong, but others, especially amateurs, were in favour of a supple stick with a heavier thong. The latter are no doubt easier to manage in a high wind, and can also be caught up with greater facility; but, in my humble opinion, the former are far preferable for general use, a supple stick and a heavy thong being insufferable in wet weather.

In the selection of a whip it is easy to observe whether the person selecting is an old hand or not. If he is he will pick out a crop without knots, or with as few as possible, whereas the tyro is nearly sure to take the knotty one. The large knots, of course, tend to keep the thong, when caught, from slipping down towards the hand, but it ought to be caught tight enough to stay in its proper place without them, and sticks always break first at the knots.

Some people are now in favour of long crops. I fancy a cricketer might as well demand a bat of extra length. In old days W. and T. Ward, who were by odds the best whipmakers, never thought of turning out whips with crops of greater length than five feet two or three inches to the holder, and most were not quite so long. Beyond this length it becomes almost impossible to obtain a good balance. A very long stick must be top heavy, and I will defy anyone to use a long top heavy whip as effectually as one that is of a more handy length.

Even when the cattle were good, and but little whip was required, thongs soon became rotten from the sweat of the horses and the rain, and to avoid the frequent necessity for new ones, what were called "three quarters and middles" were made, which coachmen were generally able to splice on for themselves. Thongs also wear out more quickly if they are not kept supple, for which purpose a dressing of two-thirds hog's lard and one-third bees wax will be found very efficacious.

CHAPTER X.

THE HOLYHEAD ROAD.

I HAVE endeavoured to show in a previous chapter, on the subject of coachmen, with what rapidity the carrying business of the country increased and multiplied, but, perhaps, this may be better elucidated by taking some particular road and district, and devoting a separate chapter to the subject; and probably no better road can be selected for this purpose than that from London to Holyhead, which, judging from the amount of money and care expended upon it, one may naturally conclude was better adapted for great speed than any other, and this, I believe, really was the case. Some particular portions of other roads might have been better—for instance, the Hartford Bridge flats—and as great, or possibly still greater pace accomplished; but for the distance over which this road extended, no other could vie with it; and I will venture to say, that on no other were an equal average number of miles of fast work performed; and we must recollect that it is one thing to go very fast for a short distance, but

another to keep that pace up for the distance ·of
from one hundred miles and upwards.   Well, then, if
we take this road, and make Birmingham, the most
important town on the road, a sort of centre of a
district, we shall obtain a pretty good insight into
the subject.

The metropolis of the Midlands has always been
celebrated for its public spirit, and it has nowhere
been made more conspicuous than in the way it met
the demand for good coaches.

In the year 1823, I find there were twenty-three
coaches advertised in *Aris's Gazette* (which was the
principal medium of advertisement at that time
in the Midlands) to run out of Birmingham
to all parts of the country, though no doubt there
were others, for it would appear that some inns, from
which coaches ran, did not avail themselves of that
medium of publicity.   Probably, therefore, after
making all allowances, we shall not err much in
putting the total number at thirty.

Four years later, in 1827, the number of those
advertised had risen to no less than thirty-eight, and
making the same allowance for those not advertised,
the total can hardly be placed at less than forty-five,
an increase of fifteen in four years.   From this time
the number was steadily added to, till by the year
1835, which may be called the culminating point
(making allowances for those not advertised, of which

three occur to my memory at once—namely, the " Rocket" night, and " Triumph " day coaches, through Oxford and Henley to London, and the " Erin-go-bragh " from Liverpool, driven by Tolly, all three horsed by Mr. Waddle from the " Hen and Chickens," in New Street), there must have been at least sixty. During these years also the pace had not been neglected, as several of these new coaches travelled at great speed, and the pace of those of older standing had been increased. In the year 1826, considerable stimulus was given to speed by a great acceleration in the time of the Holyhead mail. About which time the " Union" commenced to perform the journey from Shrewsbury to London, through Birmingham and Oxford, in four hours less time. The "Oxonian" also, over the same ground, was accelerated five hours.

It will tend to exhibit the great keenness with which the competition was carried on, if I here introduce two advertisements which appeared in the newspapers during this period.

In the month of June, 1834, the following advertisement appeared in *Aris's Gazette* :—

" The ' Greyhound,' only carrying passengers and small parcels, leaves Birmingham at a quarter past nine in the evening, arriving in London at a quarter to eight on the following morning. This coach has an imperial on the roof to prevent luggage being placed there, and passengers' luggage must be sent to the office in time to be forwarded by the ' Economist.' "

An attempt was at one time made to light this coach with gas, but the practice was, I believe, discontinued. Unless it proved of very great benefit in the power of light, it had certainly one great draw- back, which was that the necessary apparatus occupied the whole front boot, causing that receptacle to be altogether useless for the carriage of parcels.

Again, in July, 1835, the following advertisement appeared in·the *Shrewsbury Chronicle* :—

" Isaac Taylor, ever grateful for the distinguished support he has received from the public, announces a new and elegant fast day coach to London, called the ' Stag,' every morning at a quarter before five, arriving at the ' Bull and Mouth,' opposite the General Post Office, at seven . the same evening. I. T. has been induced to commence running the ' Stag ' to prevent the celebrated ' Wonder ' being in any way injured by racing, or at all interfered with in the regularity which has been hitherto observed in that coach."

It will be observed here, that the " Stag " was advertised to run the distance of one hundred and fifty-four miles in fourteen hours and a quarter. Whether this pace was really intended to be always maintained may perhaps be doubtful. Probably it depended a good deal on the amount of racing with the " Nimrod," but of this more will be heard presently. For the present, however, we will retrace our steps for a few years, and take a journey or two with the " Tally-hoes," and go more into particulars than has yet been the case.

Previously to the great improvement which I have denoted in the night travelling, a great advance had been established in the day work by the three " Tally-hoes." These coaches were put on the road about the year 1823, and were among the fastest coaches in England. Why all three bore the same name I never heard, and cannot understand, unless it were with the view of intensifying the keenness of the opposition, which, as they were all on the road at the same time, was very great. I suppose, however, that it was found to create inconvenience in practice, as they were soon supplied with distinctive titles— one being designated the " Independent Tally-ho," another the " Eclipse Tally-ho," and the other the " Patent Tally-ho." They were timed at ten miles an hour, but when racing, as was frequently the case, were not particular to a mile or two, and, of course, went much faster. Indeed, on the recurrence of what may be called the coach festival, May 1st, they more than once covered the distance, one hundred and eight miles, under seven hours. The " Independent Tally-ho," started from London from the " Golden

Cross," Charing Cross, horsed by Horne as far as
Colney, and driven by Andrew Morris to Dunstable,
where the box was filled by an old friend of mine, to
whom I am indebted for assistance in compiling this
book, but whose name I am not at liberty to mention,
who also horsed it as far as Stoney Stratford. Out
of Birmingham it started from the " Nelson," horsed
by Radenhurst, and driven to Daventry and back by
Harry Tresslove, who was an excellent waggoner,
and always galloped the five-mile stage between
Dunchurch and the " Black Dog" in eighteen minutes.
The road was straight, hard, and flat, and ran
between a splendid avenue of trees—perhaps some
of the finest elms in the world—the property of Lord
John Scott. The stage was horsed by the landlord
of the " Bell," at Dunchurch, who could afford to do
the work well, as he reaped the benefit of the coach
breakfasting at his house on the up journey, and
dining there on the down one.

The " Eclipse Tally-ho " was horsed out of Ludlow
on one side by Mrs. Mountain, from the " Saracen's
Head," Snow Hill, and consequently sometimes called
" Mountain's Tally-ho," and on the other side by
Chaplin, from the " Swan with Two Necks," Lad Lane,
as far as Colney, and driven by Tom Boyce, who also
horsed it over twenty-five miles of the lower ground.
It was horsed out of Birmingham by Waddle.

The " Patent Tally-ho " ran from the " Belle

J.Sturgess del. et lith.

M&N.Hanhart imp.

GALLOPED THE FIVE MILE STAGE, IN EIGHTEEN MINUTES.

Sauvage," Ludgate Hill, and horsed by Robert Nelson as far as South Mimms, and was driven out of London by old Bob Flack, who also horsed twenty-five miles of the lower ground.

It will be observed that a change had come over coaching, in that the coachmen were covering a good many stages of the lower ground. Probably this arose partly from the innkeepers, now that the opposition had become so exceedingly keen, not caring for the business, and also partly from the great change which had taken place in their social position and character. They were become quite a different class of persons to what they had been a generation before, and, indeed, such might be expected to be the case, as the occupation was one which brought them into contact with gentlemen, and it was entirely their own faults if they derived no benefit from such association. The pace, in consequence of the severe competition, had also become so severe that the old style of coachman, who had been accustomed to take it easy, and stop at most of the roadside inns he passed, and got half-seas over before arriving at the end of the journey, could no longer be employed, and their places had to be filled with an altogether different class of men. Indeed, it was no longer the disgusting work, in which he was most esteemed who could hit the hardest, and had for its supporters only the lower grades of

society, but had become one which no gentleman
need be ashamed to be occupied in, or have lost
his self-respect by embracing; and, doubtless, if coaching had not been supplanted by railways, the press
of competition, which is felt by all classes, would
have induced more of them to turn their attention
to it.

In new countries, such as our colonies, what a
man's employment is, so long as it is honest and
respectable, goes for little or nothing, provided he is
a gentleman in every sense of the word. He may
drive a bullock dray in the morning, and associate
with the *élite* in the evening—at least, so it was when
I knew Australia a "long time ago," which would
appear to be a better system than our own more
exclusive one. Probably, however, it would be impossible to carry it out in an old and wealthy country
like that in which we live.

The dust kicked up by the Tally-hoes was not
long laid in Birmingham before the three Shrewsbury
coaches came bustling through the town on their
journey to London. Of these the "Wonder" probably had the most world-wide fame of any coach in
England. It set the fashion of day coaches running
long distances, and was the first ever established to
cover much above one hundred miles in a day,
the distance from London to Shrewsbury being one
hundred and fifty-four; and it was unrivalled in

its punctuality. It was horsed by Sherman out of London, from the "Bull and Mouth" to St. Albans, to which place he worked most of his coaches on that road, though he extended the distance in the case of one Birmingham night coach for some time as far as Daventry, a distance of seventy-four miles. Whether this was done because he considered it too good a thing to part with, or that it was so poor a concern that no one would join him in it, I do not know. The "Wonder" was driven out of London by Wood as far as Redbourn, from whence Harry Liley worked till he met John Wilcox, when they both turned back; and between Birmingham to Shrewsbury, Sam Hayward occupied the box. I need hardly say that on such a coach, which was the pride of the road, they were all first-rate artists.

The "Wonder" was allowed to enjoy the fruits of its enterprise, and to go on its way unmolested for several years; but by the year 1830, or thereabouts, its success as a good loading coach tempted opposition, and the "Nimrod" was called into existence. It started from London on alternate days from the "Bull Inn," Holborn, and the "Belle Sauvage," Ludgate Hill, horsed from the former by Horne, and from the latter by R. Nelson, and worked by them, side by side, to Redbourn, and driven by my old friend already mentioned on the "Independent Tally-ho," who drove it to near Stoney Stratford and back, making a drive of one hundred miles a day. On one occasion, in consequence of the up coach being delayed by a broken pole, he was obliged to drive on till he met it below Daventry, which lengthened the day's work to about one hundred and seventy miles without a rest.

This distance is, I think, one of the longest ever driven at one time. Mr. Kenyon has been known to drive the "Wonder" the whole journey from London to Shrewsbury, which is nearly equal; but I fancy it has seldom if ever been exceeded, except by the memorable drive of Captain Barclay, who undertook for a bet to drive two hundred, and won it. But to return to the "Nimrod."

The opposition of these two coaches was, as one would have thought, fierce enough, but it was not sufficient to satisfy the wounded feelings of the "Wonder" proprietors, who were indignant at anyone presuming to oppose the coach of which they were so justly proud. After a few years, therefore, the "Stag" was ushered in by the glowing advertisement I have given in a previous page. It was started to run a little in front of the "Nimrod," which was followed by the "Wonder," and was therefore pretty well nursed. The orders given to the "Nimrod" coachman were, if the "Wonder" pressed to keep first, which caused him of course to run into the "Stag," and then, as may well be imagined, the racing became somewhat exciting, and the "Wonder," we may rely upon it, did not always act up to the pacific course laid down for her in the advertisement, and the result was that the three coaches sometimes arrived all together at the "Peacock" at Islington two hours before time. Perhaps the greatest wonder would have been if a coachman had been found who would not have joined in the fun when it was going on under his eyes.

When the proprietors found they could not kill one another by racing, they tried the suicidal plan of cutting down fares, which were reduced, between London and Birmingham, from two pounds eight shillings inside to thirty shillings, and outside from thirty shillings to one pound. This, coupled with the wear and tear of horse flesh caused by the pace, was, of course, ruinous, and one of them told me that he lost fifteen hundred pounds in a little over twelve months by it. Why an agreement could not have been come to whereby the coaches should have run at different times seems to be a puzzle. One would have supposed that it would have answered better for them to have set out with an hour or two between them, which would have afforded better accommodation to the public. I can only imagine one reason which actuated them, which is, that every traveller would have taken the first coach as long as there was room for him in it, for fear of the others being full, and so the first would have had an undue advantage, and little or nothing might have been left for the last.

There was also another fast night coach between London and Birmingham, called the "Emerald," driven out of the latter place by Harry Lee, whose complexion was of a very peculiar colour, almost resembling that of a bullock's liver, the fruit of strong potations of "early purl" or "dog's nose," taken after the exertions of the night and before going to roost.

Besides all the coaches I have named, the Oxford road was not neglected. The well-known "Tantivy" commenced running over it between Birmingham and London about the year 1832, and must have proved successful, for in 1835 the same proprietors put on another fast day coach, called the "Courier," to start at a quarter before seven in the morning, and precede the old-established coach, which started two hours later.

There was also a third road between the great Metropolis and that of the Midlands which ran through Warwick, Banbury, and Buckingham, and which was traversed by the Birmingham mail, and, if I recollect right, also by a night coach called the "Crown Prince."

It was not, however, on the London roads only that coaches increased and multiplied, for in the year 1834 the "Fairtrader" commenced running to Liverpool, and three other new coaches were advertised in other directions—namely, the "Red Rover" to Brecon, the "Beehive" to Manchester, and the "Criterion" to Chester.

At this time, there was also an exceedingly keen opposition between Birmingham and Derby. One of the coaches was horsed and driven by Captain Baring, and the other was horsed by Stovin and driven by Captain Douglas, who has been already mentioned as piloting the Sheffield mail. He was a most determined fellow, and stood at nothing. Indeed, the animosity between these two Jehus was quite alarming when they encountered one another, and at last became so intense that they resorted to the dangerous expedient of crossing one another, which, on one occasion, caused Douglas to run into Baring's coach, thereby causing a smash and bruising several passengers, but very fortunately none were seriously injured. This is the only instance I ever knew of coachmen driving opposition coaches entertaining a personal animosity for one another.

And now we have arrived at the last coach which was put on the road between London and Birmingham. In the year 1837 a very fast day mail was started to run to Birmingham and to go on to Crewe, where it transferred mails and passengers to the railway for conveyance to Liverpool, and was

largely patronised by Irish M.P.'s, as it ran in
connection with the packet to the Sister Isle, and
booked through. Half a dozen of those notables of
the day could frequently be seen travelling by her at
one time. It was timed at twelve miles an hour. It
was horsed by Sherman of the " Bull and Mouth "
out of London, and was driven by H. Liley, who had
long experience on the " Wonder " over the lower
ground. At Redbourn, he was replaced on the box
by my before-mentioned friend as having driven both
the " Independent Tally-ho " and afterwards the
" Nimrod," and he drove till he met the up coach
tooled by Jonathan Morris, when they changed, each
one returning to the place from which he started,
and it was taken into Birmingham by T. Liley, a
brother of Harry. He had previously driven the
" Eclipse Tally-ho," and Jonathan Morris had had his
experience upon the " Hibernia," already mentioned
as running between Liverpool and Cheltenham. He
was pitted on that coach against Jordan, who drove
the " Hirondelle," and was noted as a " butcher," but
was possessed of great strength and had adamantine
nerve, and only a first rate practitioner had a chance
with him. Jonathan was quite a different class of
coachman, and saved his stock as well as the pace
and load would allow him, and I have myself seen
him trot by Jordan in ascending the Wyle Cop in
Shrewsbury, when the latter had nearly flogged his

horses to a standstill. Perhaps I should add, in fairness to Jordan, that, though he had a beautiful team, it was composed of light horses, and that the other coach was drawn by horses possessing more size and power for enabling them to get a load up a steep ascent. I have been particular in giving the antecedents of these coachmen, as, of course, they were picked out as especially qualified for the great pace at which this mail was timed, and it was a feather in their caps. Indeed, it may be said that, as at that time the end of coaching was within measurable distance, they represented " the survival of the fittest."

About this time the Postmaster-General started several day mails besides the one just mentioned. There was one on the Brighton road, and one between Birmingham and Shrewsbury, which left the Holyhead road at Shiffnal, and, passing through Ironbridge, joined it again about four miles from Shrewsbury, and probably there were others of which I have no cognizance.

CHAPTER XI.

THE BRIGHTON ROAD.

So much has already been written about the Brighton road that, perhaps, it may seem presumptuous in me to re-open the subject, but as I have noticed the Birmingham road, I will venture to dwell very shortly upon the Brighton one, as they may be said to have been the antithesis to each other, much in the same way as now the business of the southern railways differs from that of what are called by way of distinction the heavy lines. No observant person can, I think, arrive in London from the south and drive through town straight to one of the large railway stations in the north, without being struck with the difference of the traffic. So it was in the coaching days; on one road business was paramount, on the other a little time for pleasure could be indulged in. I do not mean to say that they carried on the old practice of throwing away ten minutes or a quarter of an hour at each change of horses; far from it. The work was admirably done, but it had not about it the severe utilitarianism which was the prevailing feature with the other. The horses on the northern road showed, as a rule, more blood, and the coaches gave the idea of their having been built with a view to carrying loads at a high rate of speed. Nothing seemed wanting to ensure pace with safety, whilst, at the same time, there was nothing to lead anyone to suppose for a moment that they were anything but stage coaches.

On the other hand, on the road to the fashionable watering-place, some of the coaches, from the small amount of lettering upon them, and bright pole chains, might at first sight have been mistaken for private drags.

Notwithstanding all this pace, it must not be supposed that a journey by one of those fast coaches on the northern road was a hurried, uncomfortable day's work, with no time to eat a comfortable meal. On the contrary, though only twenty-five minutes were allowed for dinner, so much assistance was generally given in waiters to carve and wait upon the passengers, that a by no means bad dinner could be made in the allotted time; and to show that the food was not otherwise than palatable, I may instance the case of a medical gentleman residing at Brickhill (I think), but, at any rate, in the town where the up "Wonder" dined, who, whenever possible, went in with the passengers and made his dinner with them.

I will now venture on a few circumstances and

anecdotes connected with the Brighton road, which
may help to portray the differences I have been
describing in the two roads ; but, before doing so, I
should like to remark that anyone writing at this time
on the subject is liable to make mistakes, as those
coaches in some cases changed hands, as, for instance,
at one time the "Age" was the property of and driven
by Mr. Stevenson, and at a later period was in the
possession of Sir St. Vincent Cotton.   Of this coach
it has been written by Nimrod that " Mr. Stevenson
had arrived at perfection in his art and had introduced
the phenomenon of refinement into a stage coach."   I
never happened to see this coach in his time, but can
well remember Sir St. Vincent Cotton on the box of
his neat brown coach, with bright pole chains.   A
friend of mine says, "Well I remember Harry
Stevenson, with his beautiful team, starting from the
'White Horse Cellars,' and calling for his box
passenger at the United Service Club, and from
thence to the 'Elephant and Castle,' the final stop
before departure for Brighton, and his guard, George
Carrington, who was the essence of neatness and
politeness to his passengers."

This coach was for a short time driven by Sackville
Gwynne, who ran through all his property, and died in
Liverpool, where he was driving a cab.

It would be tedious to enumerate half the coaches,
nearly thirty in number, which ran out of Brighton

every day, and many of them the best looking turns-
out in the kingdom. A few as specimens will suffice.
First and foremost came the "Times," starting at
seven in the morning, arriving at Charing Cross at
twelve, and returning to Brighton at two, driven
by Sam Goodman. Bob Brackenbury, a first-rate
amateur whip at that time, used to drive from
Brighton to Sam Goodman's farm, a distance of
eleven miles, and back again in the evening. Then
there was the "Dart," another up and down coach,
driven by Bob Snow, a first-rate artist. Some may
even now remember his rubicund face, which he had
just helped to colour with a pint of sherry after his
dinner, as he mounted his box like a workman, when
returning from the "Spread Eagle," Gracechurch
Street, with his faultless drab great-coat, and a bale of
white muslin round his neck; and such top boots!
The "Elephant and Castle" was his first stopping-
place, to meet the West End branch coach; and here
he always replenished his inner man with a glass of
hot brandy and water with a spoonful of ground
ginger in it, as he said, to assist his digestion. After
he started from there, it was woe-betide the poor
horse that offended him before he reached Reigate,
where the "Dart" stopped for dinner, and in those days
the city merchants and stockbrokers knew how to
take care of themselves. His only opponent was
the "Item," driven by Charles Newman, who was

always wretchedly horsed, and could not come near him.

Another well known face on this road was that of John Willan, who, after having lost a good fortune on the turf, started the "Arrow," which was also horsed by Horne and Sam Goodman. This coach was mostly supported by the *élite* of the sporting world. The turn-out was altogether most unique.

The late Duke of Beaufort had some horses at work on this road at one time. He horsed a coach called the "Quicksilver," and Bob Pointer was the coachman (one of the best waggoners in England). He drove till he met Charley Harker half way, and then turned back. One very fine day the Duke went, as was not unusual, with some friends to see the "Quicksilver" start from the Red Office, and there found our friend Bob, not in the most upright position, just about to take hold of the ribbons from the off-wheeler's back. As soon as his Grace saw how matters stood he took them out of his hands, and drove up till he met the other coach, which he drove back, and after kicking the passengers handed the money to Bob, telling him not to let him see him in that state again. The warning, however, was not attended to for long, for, although the best of coachmen, he was a very wet 'un.

I will now ask the reader to fancy himself for a

moment transported by the touch of Columbine's wand into the Midlands, and set down in the fashionable town of Cheltenham, which, fifty years ago, was justly famed for its fast and well-appointed coaches, as well as for its health-giving waters. Though situated far inland it was, like Brighton, very much dependent on the same element for its prosperity, and was frequented by much the same class of people, though the efficacy of the waters at one place depended upon external, and at the other upon internal application. Still they resembled one another in drawing together a society of persons who had little or no occupation except that of either bathing in or drinking the water.

The High Street of Cheltenham presents now a very different aspect to what it did at the time I am writing about, when the seats on the sunny side were occupied by visitors looking at the coaches passing to and fro or turning into the " Plough " yard. It was a sight worth coming for to see those well-horsed coaches. There were, first, the London coaches arriving : the " Magnet," driven by Jemmy Witherington, and the " Berkely Hunt," with Frank Martindale on the box, who was always the pink of neatness—indeed, as he once said to me a good many years afterwards, " You know, I was a bit of a dandy in those days."

Then there was also the London day mail with four greys, running alternately to the " Plough " and

"Queen's Hotel," and later on in the day the "Hirondelle," driven by Finch, a rather wet soul, and the "Hibernia," arrived from Liverpool, both of which coaches are incidentally mentioned in another chapter, and were two of the fastest in England. Besides them, there were others running to Bath, Bristol, Leamington, Birmingham, and other places, and by the time all these had been inspected, it was time to think of dinner.

And now, having already made this chapter something of a "fugitive piece," I will, for the second time, make use of the fairy wand, and by one of its miraculous touches translate us back again to the Brighton road, which, being the one on which so many amateurs have become professionals, may be not inappropriately called the border land between them, and, therefore, as rather pointed out for considering the difference between them. Of course, in one sense, the demarcation is as plain as the nose on one's face. The man who drives for pay is a professional, at any rate for a time; but the question I would now raise is not that, but one more likely to prove an apple of discord—I mean what allowance should be made between them in estimating their proficiency in driving. What might be good for one might be decidedly under the mark for the other. To more fully explain my meaning, I will take a strong case. Sir St. Vincent Cotton, as is well known, drove professionally for some years on the Brighton road after having been acknowledged to be a first-rate amateur, and the question is, how soon after taking to the box professionally could he have been expected to pass muster with the professionals ? Perhaps some will say that he was quite as good a coachman before as after he took to the bench professionally. No doubt his is a strong case, and I only give it as one in point ; but, for myself, I very much doubt whether, even in those *coachy* days, it was possible for a man to get sufficient practice, only as an amateur, to make him equal to one who drove professionally.

Doubtless, among the professionals there were men who never with any amount of practice became good coachmen ; but then we must remember that in all classes and conditions of men some are to be found who, from indolence or taking no pride in their work, never even reach mediocrity, whilst others are too conceited to learn ; but these were in a small minority, and in driving, as in all other crafts, practice makes perfect. If it confers no other benefit, it must strengthen the muscles, and, no doubt, imparts a handiness, readiness, and resource which nothing else can produce. The difference is, perhaps, oftener to be observed in the whip hand than the rein one. A well-practised professional with a pair of sluggish leaders will make every cut tell, and then bring the thong up to his hand without staring about to see where the wind had blown it to; whereas, it would too often be the case with an amateur that, for want of having had sufficient practice, half his cuts fell flat, and not unfrequently, especially on a windy or wet day, he will get hung up in some part of the harness or in the pole chains, or possibly even round the stock of the wheel.

It is not only in the art of driving that this difference is to be met with, but it extends to huntsmen and jockeys. In neither of these occupations does a gentleman attain to sufficient proficiency to be called more than a good amateur, which implies that he is not equal to a professional, or at any rate to a good one. Now, why is this? Surely not because he was born a gentleman, and is, therefore, disqualified by nature. Still less, because education has unfitted him. No—it is simply because he does not give up his time to it, but only follows it as a recreation. Cricket might, perhaps, at first sight, contradict this rule, but in truth, I believe it only tends to confirm it. The gentlemen are able to hold their own with the players, but then, whilst the cricket season lasts, they work as hard as the professionals.

To come to the point, then, how soon after taking to the bench professionally ought an amateur to cease to claim any indulgence in criticism? I do not, of course, mean a muff, whose natural inaptitude might render him proof against any amount of practice, but one called "a good amateur whip ; " and, probably, it would not be erring much to say that a period of from one to two years, with sixty to eighty miles of driving a day, including a fair share of night work, is sufficient to land him at the top of the profession, if the *gift* is in him.

Talking of the "gift," reminds me of a conversation which once took place between the late Mr. J. Taylor, who kept the "Lion" yard in Shrewsbury, and the well known "Chester Billy." They had been talking on the subject of driving, and the latter finished it by saying, " Well, master, it is a gift," to which the other replied, " It is, Billy, and it's a pity you never got it." I need hardly say, the old man turned away rather disgusted, and, no doubt, with the firm conviction that his master was no judge.

Perhaps, in opposition to what I have said, I may be directed to some instances where very fine samples of driving have been executed by gentlemen. I will only mention two of them. The first took place in times long ago, and is thus described by Nimrod. "Perhaps one of the finest specimens of good coachmanship was performed by Sir Felix Agar. He made a bet, which he won, that he would drive his own four horses in hand up Grosvenor Place, down the passage into Tattersall's yard, around the pillar which stands in the centre of it, and back again into Grosvenor Place, without either of the horses going at a slower pace

than trot." So long a time has expired since this feat
was performed, and all spectators have passed away,
that it is impossible to criticise it in any way. Many,
however, must be still alive who remember the old
Tattersall's, and they will be able to appreciate the
difficulty of the task.

The other is quite of a recent date, only
occurring last summer, and was performed by my
friend, Mr. Pryce Hamilton, who was the victor in
the obstacle competition. Not having seen this, I am
unable to say anything about it, but make no doubt
that those who laid out the course did not err on the
side of leniency to the coachmen, and that it was a
feat of no easy performance. But, then, these things
are hardly tests of every day coachmanship. No
doubt they require very neat handling of the reins,
but, of course, the horses have individually the best
of manners, and the teams are as hardy as it is
possible to make them ; but if the whip had been
wanted in Tattersall's yard, perhaps Sir Felix might
have lost his bet.

Perhaps, it may be thought by some that the time
I have stated is an unnecessarily long apprenticeship.
It may be for some, but for myself, I can answer that,
whether from natural stupidity or not, it was no more
than I required. Driving, if by that is understood a
perfect knowledge of the art, is, like most other
things, a plant of slow growth, and, to any one who

has given much thought and attention to it, it is surprising how long he finds something to learn. For myself, although I had done many hundreds of miles of spare work for different coachmen, and out of different yards, with the approval of the proprietors, I did not find that I had been able to overcome shortcomings and defects, of which I was conscious, till I had driven regularly for three summers, and, perhaps, even then many remained of which I was unconscious.

If there are any who think there is no difference between amateur and professional coachmen, I would ask them why there was not one of the owners of the "Old Times" put up to drive the justly celebrated match instead of Selby?

CHAPTER XII.

EARLY DAYS.

THOUGH it is rather a singular coincidence that my earliest experiences should be laid in the same neighbourhood as has been more than once mentioned by the late Mr. Birch Reynardson in " Down the Road," if the incidents are different, I suppose it will not signify much if the road is the same.

I have no recollection that we ever did actually drive opposition to one another, but it is not impossible that we may have done so, as I was in the habit of driving the " Royal Oak," which he mentions as running opposition to the " Nettle," on which coach he frequently handled the ribbons. However this may be, I can recollect well that he bore the character of a good, powerful coachman, and I only hope I may be able to approach him at all in my powers of description.

His spirited narratives carry one's thoughts back to scenes of a kindred nature, after a lapse of half a century, nearly as fresh as if it were only yesterday. For, reader, I am another old coachman, having driven one coach ninety-three miles a-day during one summer, and have worked another about fifteen thousand miles a-year for three years, besides others for myself, or for other coachmen.

I well recollect the "yard of tin"; indeed, when a youth, I possessed one, and flattered myself I could blow it pretty well. Such, indeed, was my passion for the road, that I was not satisfied till I could perform every feat performed by coachmen or guards. To pass from the back of the coach to the front, or *vice versa,* was sometimes accomplished by guards, and, of course, I must do the same, creeping between the hind wheel and the body, whilst the coach was proceeding at the rate of ten miles an hour. This was not a very easy performance, but to get up and down whilst the coach was in motion was not at all difficult, and doing this once led to my being mistaken for a professional guard.

I was travelling through North Wales, from Oswestry to Bangor, by a pair-horse coach, which, of course, did not aspire to much pace, and, as the day was wet, the road was heavy, which brought the two-horse power to a walk up some of the hills, slight as Mr. Telford's engineering skill had made them. Upon these occasions I got down to walk, and as my pace was faster than that of the horses, I was part way down the next hill before they overtook me, when, motioning to the coachman not to pull up, I returned to my seat by his side, and after having done this once

or twice he said, " I beg your pardon, sir, but were
you ever a guard on any coach ? "

It is somewhat strange that Mr. Reynardson and
I should both have good reason for remembering the
Llanymynech toll-bar, but its existence was nearly
being impressed on my mind by a far more serious
accident than killing poor piggy.

Many years ago, about the year 1836, before I had
the honour of wearing His Majesty's uniform, I used
to indulge my love of driving by starting from my
father's house, about three miles from Welshpool,
about five o'clock in the morning, and walking to that
town for the pleasure of driving the " Royal Oak "
coach, which started at six, and returning the same
day by the down coach.   Thereby getting a drive of
about eighty miles, and the pace was fast, especially if
the " Nettle " was supposed to be near, for we knew
by experience that it followed very quickly; so there
was pretty well enough of practice to be had.

On one of these mornings, when we were about
two miles on our journey, Harry Booth, the coachman,
who was sitting by my side, whistled to the horses,
which started them off beyond my powers of holding
them.   I said, " For goodness' sake be quiet," when he
coolly replied, " I thought you wanted to drive."   Fortunately, however, they came back to me after going a
short distance, and we completed the nine miles to
Llanymynech in thirty-five minutes from the start.

This was, perhaps, a rather rough way of learning to drive, and something like throwing a fellow into deep water to teach him to swim. At any rate, it taught me to gallop, and a coachman who could not do that was of little use on a good many coaches in those days.

This, however, is a digression, as it was on the return journey of that day that I nearly came to grief at the Llanymynech toll-bar. It occurred in this way—

The " Royal Oak " did not carry a guard, and Tom Loader, the coachman, having resigned his seat to me when the coaches met, had retired to the one usually occupied by that functionary. As, however, he was not accustomed to guard's work, he was deficient in the activity necessary for slipping the skid pan under the wheel whilst the coach was in motion, and when he tried to do so at the top of Llanymynech hill he failed in the attempt. Consequently, we got over the brow of the hill without the wheel being locked, and, as there were no patent breaks in those days, there was nothing for it but a gallop, as the wheel horses were unable to hold the big load of passengers and luggage, and, of course, the lurches of the coach became considerable, to say the least of it. The turnpike gate, which was at the bottom of the hill, was rather a narrow one, and a collision seemed not altogether improbable, when, just as the leaders reached the gate, the passenger sitting on the roof seat behind me became so much alarmed that he seized hold of my right arm, thereby rendering any use of the whip impossible if it had been necessary, which, fortunately, it was not, as the coach was then in a safe direction, though rather too near the off-side gate-post to be pleasant.   If the whip had been wanted to make the off-wheel horse pull us clear of the post I was helpless, and a collision would have been attended with an awful smash, as we were going at the rate of a mile in five minutes at the time. Killing the pig would have been nothing to it.

Whilst on the subject of toll gates I am reminded that I did on one occasion break one all to pieces, and, though chronologically out of place here, I am tempted to introduce it.

It occurred many years subsequently to the affair at Llanymynech, when I was residing at Aberystwith, and, as often happened whilst there, I was working the Shrewsbury and Aberystwith mail between the latter place and Newtown for one of the regular coachmen, who wanted a few days' rest.   One morning on the down journey, on our reaching the toll gate at Caersws, the gatekeeper threw it open to allow the mail to pass, but, as he did not throw it sufficiently far back to hold in the catch, the high wind blew it back again, causing it to come in contact with the stock of the near fore wheel.   Of course, it was

too late to pull up, but, fortunately, the gate was old
and very rotten, and doubled up with the collision.
It was broken all to pieces, but, with the exception of
a few slight cuts on the horses from splinters of wood,
no injury was sustained. The toll-bar man was
disposed to give some trouble, but little Rhodes, the
post-office guard (for it was one of the last mails that
carried them), shut him up with the remark that the
penalty for delaying the mails was fifty pounds.

Before taking leave of the subject of racing, such
as was carried on by the " Royal Oak " and " Nettle "
coaches, I am induced to make a few remarks about
it. Perhaps, some one on reading what I have said,
may be disposed to exclaim, " how dangerous it must
have been!" and, indeed, Mr. Reynardson says in
" Down the Road," speaking of these coaches, " they
were often too fast to be quite safe, as I sometimes
used to fancy." To this, the result of his practical
experience, I will not demur, suffice it to say that,
though I have known a coachman of the " Royal
Oak " fined for furious driving, I never knew a case
of one scattering his passengers. Of course, it was
not altogether unaccompanied by danger, but, judging
by results, it could not have been very serious, as the
accidents which occurred from it were not greater than
were produced by other causes. Indeed, there are
some reasons why they may have been less. When
coaches were running strong opposition, everything,

horses, coaches, and harness, were all of the very best, and none but real "artists" could be placed upon the box. (I think I hear a whisper that sometimes boys got there.) They were, therefore, secure from any accident caused, as was sometimes the case, by carelessness and penuriousness, which, to my own knowledge, have been productive of some very serious ones, as I shall show.

About twenty-five years ago, during one summer, two accidents occurred on the road between Dolgelly and Caernarvon, which might easily have been prevented—one of which was accompanied by serious loss of life, and which was to be attributed entirely to the use of old worn-out coaches and harness, or inferior coachmen and horses, such as, if the pace had been greater, no one would have ventured to employ. To the other accident there was a rather comic side, though not, perhaps, exactly to the sufferer. The coach was upset a few miles from Barmouth, on the road to Harlech, and the coachman's shoulder was dislocated ; whereupon, a medical practitioner, who was passing at the time, mistaking the injury for a fracture, splintered it up. This treatment, of course, did not tend to mend matters, and the shoulder continued so painful that upon arriving at Caernarvon another surgeon was called in, who perceived the real nature of the injury, and reduced the dislocation.

Then, again, as a fact, there was not so often, as

may be supposed, a neck-and-neck race with two
coaches galloping alongside of each other. Such
things did occur at times, when the road was wide
enough to admit of it ; but much oftener the coachmen did not try to give one another the "*go-bye*,"
except when the leading one was called upon to stop
to pick up or put down a passenger, or for any other
purpose. It was understood that on those occasions,
if the opposition was close behind, the one which
stopped should pull to his own side of the road, leaving
space to pass. Then the other one, getting in front,
would " *spring 'em*," to try, if possible, to complete his
next change of horses and be off again without being
passed.

No coachman, who knew his business, or was not
utterly reckless, would think of racing down hill,
though occasionally, no doubt, they did take liberties
at the top of a hill and come to grief. There could,
however, be no danger in trying to pass when ascending
a hill, and then was the opportunity for the coachman
with the lightest load or strongest team to challenge
his opponent. Of course, the leading one would not
give his rival the road if he could help it, and I have
had my near-side leader's bar rattling against his off-
side hind wheel before he would give me room to
pass ; but there was no danger involved in that, as,
being on the ascent, I could have pulled up at any
moment.

As to there being any danger in merely galloping a coach, I am sure there is not, even at a high speed, provided the wheel horses are well matched in stride, the team well put together, and kept well in hand, and when there is sufficient draught to keep the leaders' traces tight.   This will be apparent from the fact that, however much a coach may have been lurching previously, as soon as the leaders commence drawing, she becomes perfectly steady.   Of course with the pole chains too slack there would be danger.

Then, again, the build of the coach has a good deal to do with it.   For very fast work, coaches were generally kept what was called near the ground. Those which were built by Shackleford, of Cheltenham, for the " Hirondelle," which raced with the " Hibernia," between that town and Liverpool, at a pace as great if not greater than any coaches in England, were contracted to be made so that the roof should not exceed a certain height from the ground.   I forget now what the exact measurement was, but it was some inches less than the general build, and to enable this to be done the perch was slightly bent.

The "Hibernia" coaches also, which were supplied by Williams, of Bristol, were admirably adapted for the work they had to perform, being low and remarkably steady, but heavier than those of their opponent.   Indeed, Williams's coaches were not favourites with coachmen on account of their weight, but as they were generally contracted for by the mile, those were most profitable to the contractor that required the least repairs. I have heard of a coachman complaining to Mr. Williams about the weight of his coaches, to which the laconic answer was a five-shilling piece, and " Don't you bother about that."

These two coaches always made the first of May a day for more than ordinary racing, and performed the journey on those occasions at a very accelerated pace. I am afraid, at this distance of time, to say exactly by how much the time was shortened, but certainly by two or three hours, and as the ordinary time was twelve hours and a half to cover the distance of one hundred and thirty-three miles, the pace must have been very severe.

On one of these annual festivals there was a lady travelling inside the "Hirondelle," and one of the proprietors, thinking she might be alarmed at the terrific pace the coach was going at, offered to "post her" the remainder of the journey without extra charge. She, however, was quite equal to the occasion, and replied that she was much obliged by the offer, but that she liked going fast. This showed well, not only for her nerve, but also that the driving was good, and that the coachmen "made their play" judiciously.

CHAPTER XIII.

OLD TIMES.

IT may seem strange to those who have never had any experience of road travelling, that the memory of hours spent in journeys, when the passengers by public conveyances had only the choice between passing a whole day, and still more, a night, exposed to all the vicissitudes of the British climate, or else in what, compared even to a third-class carriage on a railway, was little better than a box upon wheels, should conjure up reminiscences of happy hours passed under circumstances which must naturally appear to those who have never tried it, absolutely insufferable. Such, however, I believe to be the case, and I very much doubt whether anything like the same affectionate reminiscences will linger about the present luxurious mode of travelling.

At the present age, in consequence of the generally increased luxury, there has arisen an impatience of discomfort unknown to previous generations. Whether this arises from the fact that journeys are now so soon accomplished that one never feels it

necessary to try and make the best of it, and affords
no opportunity for a trial of pluck and endurance,
dear to the heart of an Englishman, I know not ; but
that there is something deeply seated in human nature,
which takes delight in recounting what it has gone
through in the way of suffering is certain ; or, perhaps,
it may be that there was something which addressed
itself to the love of sport, innate to man, in travelling
behind four horses. This point I will not venture to
decide. Certain it is that coaching has always been
supposed to be nearly related to sporting. In the
daytime, especially in fine weather, there is something
very exhilarating in passing quickly through the air,
and hearing the rapid steps of four horses on the hard
road ; and then there was, at least by day, just time
enough, even on the fastest coaches, to run into the
bar occasionally, whilst the horses were being changed,
to have a glass of brown sherry, and exchange a word
and a laugh with the pretty barmaid—for they were
all pretty ! At any rate, these things helped to break
the monotony of the journey. Again, if the traveller
desired to become acquainted with the country he
was passing through, he could be in no better place for
seeing it than on the outside of a coach, which by
passing through the towns on the route afforded a
much better idea of what they were like in architecture
and other things, than by only skirting them, as must
necessarily be the case on a railway. I often fancy

that entering a town from a railway station is something like sneaking into a house by the back door. Night travelling, no doubt, had its serious drawbacks, but they were, to some extent at least, alleviated by a stoppage of sufficient time to get a good supper, such as would warm up the cockles of the heart, and enable the passengers to start again warm, and with a fresh stock of pluck to endure what they could not cure. At any rate, they knew no better.

I tell my grandson that he loses twelve hours of his holidays from Eton now, since he does not have what I look back upon as a downright jolly night. Instead of not leaving college till the morning of breaking up as at present, the " Rocket " coach of the old days, from London to Birmingham and Shrewsbury, used on the previous evening to come to Slough empty, where it arrived about seven o'clock, and at which place we boys who were going long journeys in that direction were allowed to join it ; and right well we filled it, inside and out, though the latter was the most coveted position, as being thought more manly. I recollect on my second journey home, though it was the Christmas holidays, my anxious parents having secured an inside place for me, I exchanged it with another boy, "without receiving the difference," so that I might not travel inside, and after that I was left to my own choice.

As it was known some days before what the load

would be composed of on those nights, an extra good supper was provided at Oxford, to which we did ample justice, and, as the coach was pretty much at our service on that occasion, there was time to enjoy ourselves thoroughly, which we did to our hearts' content, and started off again warm and comfortable and as "jolly as sand-boys," though I must admit we did know what cold feet were before arriving at Birmingham about eight o'clock on the following morning. That, however, coach travellers expected, and would, perhaps, have been rather disappointed without it.

On these nights the coach used to be so heavily loaded with luggage that things were hung to the lamp-irons, and everything else that could be pressed into the service, and on one sharp, frosty night some small articles were slung under the hind axle, amongst which was a basket of fish; unfortunately, this had been allowed to hang so low down that it came in contact with the hard, frosty road, and when the place was reached where it was to be delivered, nothing could be found but the basket with the bottom out, the cod and oysters having been scattered on the road.

The " Rocket " was not so fast a coach as its name might imply, and old Rook, who drove one side between Birmingham and Shrewsbury, though a good coachman of the old school, was not very particular to ten minutes or so, but would sometimes stop and

take a little pleasure on the road; and I well remember passing through Bilson when a bull was
being baited on a piece of open ground between the
houses, and close to the roadside, and he pulled up to
watch the operations for some time. There was a
story told of him, that he had a friend who was a pig
dealer, whose business frequently caused him to be
walking in the same direction as the coach, and if
there was room he would give him a lift. One day
he came up with his friend walking at his very best
pace, when, as usual, he offered him a ride, to which
he replied, "No thank you, old fellow, not to-day; I
am in a hurry, and can't while."

I cannot say that the return journey carries with
it the same pleasurable recollections, even after this
distance of time. The "Triumph" coach by which
it was performed, was a night one between Shrewsbury and Birmingham, and travelled by day above the
latter town, but as it had only a pair of horses up to
there it was a very slow affair, starting from Shrewsbury at eleven o'clock at night, and not arriving at
Birmingham before six on the following morning.
To send a boy back to school on a two-horse power,
which consumed seven hours in covering forty-four
miles, seems rather like "adding insult to injury."
The only amusement we could by any possibility
indulge in was when we came to a turnpike gate,
when the collector was sleepy and slow in opening it,

to cry out "Fire!" as loud as we could to alarm him. We found that the cry of "Murder!" had no effect.

My recollection also reminds me that we did not always travel home by the "Rocket." One Easter holidays three of us started from Eton to post to London in one of the old yellow post-chaises, when soon after passing Slough, the demon of mischief taking possession of us, we determined to have some fun on the road, for which purpose we changed half-a-crown into coppers, and using them as missiles, made a stealthy attack upon the shop windows as we drove along. This fun lasted very well till after changing horses at Hounslow, but upon passing through Brentford, whether we had become too bold and careless, or whether the inhabitants of that town were a sharper race, I don't know, but we all of a sudden found ourselves the object of much interest to them, and a man running out of a shop, seized hold of our horses' heads, and calling us all the young blackguards he could think of, presented his little account for broken glass, etc., etc. I need hardly say that this was immediately settled without haggling, and telling the post-boy to make the best of his way, we soon left the town of Brentford, and further hostile attention on the part of its inhabitants, behind us.

In the previous generation a case occurred when a journey home from Eton was performed on a much grander scale than that which I have just recorded, and as it was of necessity performed by road, may not be inappropriately introduced in this place.

The then Bishop of Worcester, Dr. Cornwall, had two sons at Eton, and on a certain Election Monday they started to go home to their paternal mansion at Diddlesbury, situate in Corvedale in the county of Salop, where the Bishop resided a good deal of his time. The family temper was of rather a hasty nature, and something occurred after the young gentlemen had proceeded a certain distance on the journey which stirred up this hereditary failing, the altercation becoming so strong that they parted company, each one ordering out a post-chaise and four for his own individual use; and it ended in first of all one of them arriving at his destination in a post-chaise and four from Ludlow, followed in about a quarter-of-an-hour by the other brother in a similar conveyance. Report does not say how the Right Rev. father received his sons, but if he had a spice of the family temper, he probably gave them a "*mauvais quart d'heure*," as the Frenchman says. At any rate, one thing is certain, that it would puzzle the picturesque little town of Ludlow at the present time to turn out "*two fours*" without a long warning.

CHAPTER XIV.

COACHMEN : WHERE DID THEY COME FROM?

COACHMEN, as they used to be, are now nearly, or quite, lost to sight, and it is difficult to describe them. Most of the descriptions given of them have been, more or less, caricatures ; still, from the time of Tony Weller, they have been a rather peculiar people, although that character, as depicted by Dickens, was more in keeping with a previous generation, and even highly coloured for that, and as unlike what they were in the palmy days of coaching as were two men I saw at Hatchett's a summer or two ago, dressed in such great-coats as were never seen down any road, and with such hats upon their heads as, I should think, never made their appearance anywhere, unless it was on the stage. They were a sort of Gog and Magog of the road.

The coachman of the fastest and best days, which really lasted for a comparatively small number of years, was better educated, and was rarely slangy in his dress, which was well suited to his avocation, and, except in winter, would not generally attract attention.

At that season, however, he did require to be well
protected against weather, for he had to face all sorts,
and that for nearly a whole day or night at a time.
On one journey the rain might fall incessantly, on
another our changeable climate would produce clear
weather accompanied by intense frost, whilst on the
following day there might be a driving snow, the wind
blowing the flakes into the eyes till it was almost
impossible to see the road.

Now all these alternations of weather had to be
taken into account, and, I believe, the art of resisting
them had well-nigh reached perfection ; therefore, with
the dread before my eyes of wearying some of my
readers, I am tempted to enter with some minuteness
into the subject, as, judging from the garments now
usually worn, the art is lost in the present day. It was
a well established fact that two moderately thick coats
gave more warmth and kept out wet better than one
which was very thick, and besides which, a very thick
coat becomes insufferably heavy after being out many
hours in the rain.

Indeed, a great change had taken place in the
dress of coachmen. As the pace increased, and better
bred horses were employed, and greater activity was
required in the coachmen, the cumbersome old great-
coat, with innumerable capes, had to make room for
garments which interfered less with the movements of
the wearer. I need hardly say to those who have

had much experience, that there is no hope of keeping
dry and warm if the neck is not secured by an ample
upper neckcloth ; for, tying up this part of the body
not only excludes the wet and cold, but also has the
effect of keeping in the natural heat of the body.
Nothing chills worse than a cold draught passing
up the sleeves and coming out at the neck, and to
prevent this what were called coachman's cuffs were
employed. These consisted of a piece of cloth about
six inches in length, which buttoned over the sleeve of
the ordinary coat, and when over these were added,
first, a strong cloth coat, and over that a waterproof
cape with sleeves, and ample enough to spread well
over the apron, no wet and little cold could penetrate.
Protected in this way, and with a relay of dry woollen
gloves and whips, a not unpleasant day might be spent
on the coach box even when the elements were
unpropitious.

When a man is cased in all these clothes, he can
hardly help being a little stiff in his movements, and
this imparted a peculiar gait which betrayed the occupation. The left hand also generally acted as a tell
tale, as the rounded position in which the wrist was
necessarily held during many hours of the day could
not be altogether thrown off at other times. It was
not uncommon for guards in the fast day coaches to
wear red coats, not the post-office guard's livery, as I
have seen at Hatchett's, but an ordinary hunting coat.

As roads improved pace increased, and fast day
coaches gradually appeared, notably the three " Tally-
hoes" between Birmingham and London, distinguished
from one another by the words " Eclipse," " Patent,"
and " Independent ; " also the " York House," Bath,
and the " Berkely Hunt," Cheltenham.

It was not, however, till about the year 1825 that
the " Wonder" commenced running between Shrewsbury and London, a distance of one hundred and fifty-
four miles, and it ceased running the whole journey
through in the year 1840 or 1841.   And this having
been the first coach which attempted to cover so long
a journey in one day, it marks with sufficient accuracy
the time during which coaching was at its zenith.   Of
course, there were many fast and good coaches running
after this date ; but subsequent to the year 1842,
most of the roads, taking their start from the
Metropolis, were, more or less, pressed upon by
railways, and the coaches were either taken off altogether, or else the distance run was curtailed.   We
may therefore put down about twenty-five years as the
period during which the coaches covered the roads,
though many equally good ones continued to run in
Scotland, Wales, and other remote places for many
years later.

During this quarter of a century the fun was fast,
not to say furious, and with such rapidity did coaches
increase and multiply, that it is a wonder how the

J. Sturgess del. et lith.

MkN. Hanhart imp.

EXTRA PAIR OF HORSES FOR FAST COACHES, FOR STEEP ASCENTS.

demand for coachmen was satisfied, for to become one
fit to be entrusted with a fast coach, and one which
loaded heavily, necessitates no little practice.

From whence then was this demand supplied?
Principally, I believe, like that in other trades, on the
hereditary principle. It was no uncommon thing for
old coachmen to have several sons at work; but, as
the box of a good day coach was a lucrative post, a
considerable number of men were gradually attracted
to it from superior positions in life. The value of a
" drive" differed very much, according to the loading
of the coach, distance driven, whether single or double
journey, or whether the passengers were what was
called "*good cloth*," or the contrary; but one which did
not bring in twenty shillings a day was not thought
much of, and some were worth double.

This may appear a large remuneration to be
received for a day's work, seldom occupying more than
nine or ten hours; but I know it is not overstated, as
I have not only been told it by others, but have myself
fingered forty-five shillings in one day. Perhaps, however, I should add that I was then driving as much as
ninety-three miles a day, and had no guard.

There were also other sources from which money
was made, and from which coachmen driving slow
coaches were enabled to make amends for the inferior
quality of their passengers; and, indeed, in quite old
days, the best wheel of the coach was often his. The

late Mr. Jobson, who for many years kept the "Talbot
Hotel" in Shrewsbury, and horsed the "Nimrod,"
which ran opposition.to the "Wonder," had previously
driven the "Prince of Wales" coach between that
town and Birmingham, during which time he had the
opportunity of buying up the guineas, when they were
called in by the Mint, at a trifle under their standard
value, and being able to dispose of them at their full
price he realised a handsome profit.

Again, fish was not an unusual article to be made
the subject of trading, and I once was tempted to
embark in this business myself, but, as the sequel
will show, not with satisfactory results. When I was
driving the "Snowdonian," I was frequently asked
by friends and acquaintances on the road to bring
some fish from Caernarvon, as the towns through
which I passed were badly supplied with it. Accordingly, one morning, hearing that a good catch of
fish had been brought in, I invested, before starting,
in forty pounds of very nice small salmon at sixpence
a pound, with the expectation of obliging friends, and
at the same time making some profit for my trouble.
However, I was soon undeceived. As I went from
place to place I announced with a feeling of much
complacency that I had got the long-wanted article,
but in most cases the answer was that they did not
want salmon — any other fish would have been
acceptable. Consequently, when I arrived at the end

of my journey, I found that more than half was left
in hand. Pickled salmon was the standard dish on
my table for a fortnight. It was my first and last
appearance in the character of a fishmonger. I tried
no other sort of fish, as I thought they were too
dainty if they could not eat salmon. But perhaps I
have digressed too far, and will return to where
coachmen sprang from in the required numbers.

I once sat by the side of a Captain Douglas, who
had seen service in the Peninsular war, and was
then driving the Birmingham and Sheffield mail
out of the former town, and a quiet, nice coachman he was. He had a long stage of sixteen miles
to Lichfield, and brought his team in fresh at the
end of it.

From the officer coachman I come to the private.
He was named Marsh, and had served at Waterloo
with the 14th Regiment, and after leaving the army,
had driven a coach between Maidstone and London
for many years. When I first became acquainted with
him, he had, like a good many others, followed the
receding tide to the west, and was driving one side
of the Aberystwith and Shrewsbury mail, between the
former place and Newtown, during which time I
occasionally worked for him; but, like an old soldier,
he was always, if possible, ready for duty. It is
curious enough that I first came across him on a
Waterloo day, when he modestly remarked, upon the

subject being alluded to, " I happened to be there."
I had lost sight of him for some years, till I observed
a notice of him in the *World* newspaper of July 11th,
1888.   It occurred in a short account of Lord
Albemarle, and mentioned the interest he took in
"the old soldier Matty Marsh, private 14th Foot,
who was wounded at Waterloo, witnessed the
funerals of Wellington and Napoleon, drove a coach
from Maidstone for many years, and recently died at
the advanced age of ninety-four years."   I never
heard him allude to either of the funerals, and don't
very well see how he could have been at that of
Napoleon's ; but so far as I know, he may have
attended both.

A few postboys were elevated to the "bench,"
notably little Dick Vickers, of the Holyhead mail ;
but few of them were equal to the task, and, indeed,
some of them could not even handle four-horse reins
sufficiently well for black work, and consequently the
night coachmen were occasionally pressed into this
service, much to their dislike, and this once led to a
rather droll scene.   A gentleman, who had taken to
professional coach driving, found himself one day
let in for the job of driving a hearse, and, of course,
was obliged to get himself up for the occasion something like a mute, when catching sight of himself
in a glass, he was so much struck with his personal
appearance, that he remarked, " Well, if only some

of my family could see me now, I wonder what they *would* say ? "

Indeed, it is difficult to determine from what ranks and professions the large body of coachmen required in those days was not recruited. I suppose few would have looked among the list of publishers for one, but, nevertheless, one, at any rate, from that business was drawn into the service of the road, not having been successful in the former trade. A letter from an old friend of mine, also a coachman, will, I think, interest or amuse some readers, and will show that he possessed a considerable amount of grim humour, as well as some acuteness in business.

"Many years ago," says my friend, "I took up my residence for a short time at the 'Kentish Hotel' in Tunbridge Wells—the best hotel there, and at that time there were very few houses built upon the Common. After stopping there some time, the season ended, and the exodus of visitors had commenced, I took the box seat on Stockdale's coach. I must tell you he had been a large publisher in Piccadilly, but failed, and then took to the road, this being the first coach he had driven, and being part proprietor. He was an exceedingly good amateur whip, but still, not a first-rate artist, as he would try to make you believe.

"A short time before we started, a lady with her maid, who had been stopping in the hotel, sent her

12

luggage to be placed on the coach, and upon Stockdale seeing it, he said to the porter, 'How many
passengers, Tom?' 'Two, sir,' says Tom. 'Scale
it, Tom,' says he, which he immediately did. When
twelve shillings was demanded for extra luggage, the
lady said, 'I never paid it before, and have taken
two inside places.' 'You see, *ma'ame*,' says he, 'I
horse this coach over Maramscote hill, and I cannot
carry your luggage for nothing; you will bring the
kitchen range next time if you have nothing
to pay.'

"Having seated myself very comfortably on the
box seat, our friend Stockdale and myself lit our
cigars, going at a fair pace till we were descending
Maramscote hill, the skid-pan being on the wheel.
The wheel horses did not step well together, and
we rocked very considerably, which led me to
observe he had better be careful, or he would put
the passengers down to count them. Upon this he
turned round to me, looking daggers, and asked me
to look what was painted on the board at the side
of the hill, and looking, I read, '*Dry rubbish may be
thrown here.*' You may be sure I did not offer any
more advice for the remainder of the stage; but our
contretemps soon cooled down, and when we were
changing horses, 'I say, governor!' says he, 'forget
the dry rubbish, and come in and take a little cold
brandy and water. It's the only place I ever go

into on the road, for it's the only place where you can escape being poisoned.' After our refreshment we went at a very jolly pace, having Robert Nelson's horses, which were first-rate, and soon arrived at the Belle Sauvage, Ludgate Hill, where we found a great bustle of coaches, and luggage just come by other coaches, arriving from different parts of the country, and porters were calling out, 'Any passengers for Leeds "Courier," "Hope," Halifax,'" etc., etc.

It was not only necessary that a coachman should be able to drive well, which required time and practice to acquire, but, what was of nearly equal importance, he had to learn how to get his coach quick through the country. Indeed, his was a position of no small responsibility, for he had the lives and limbs of the passengers in his hands, and as, when was sometimes the case with a strong opposition, his orders were simply "*be first,*" his was no very enviable situation. When he could do all this with the minimum of wear and tear of the stock, he was a very valuable man to his employers.

As a rule, I think they were fairly careful of the stock, though certainly on slow coaches, when a little time lost could be recovered without much difficulty, the horses by no means always reaped the full benefit of the time allowed them. This, however, it must with justice be admitted, was not altogether the fault of the coachmen. The proprietors were too prone

to encourage delay for the custom it brought to the
"bar," and if a coachman was heard to decline the
offer of a glass of sherry or brandy and water from
his box passenger, he might expect black looks.

Of course, with the fastest coaches, such delays
were impossible, neither could the coachman find time
to pull up and patronize the house of a friend, as was
frequently done by his brethren on the slower drags.

I have heard of the late Mr. Isaac Taylor, of
Shrewsbury, when he wanted to select from among
his coachmen one fitted for a fast coach, adopting
the following plan: One of his coaches was driven
by a man who he knew to be coachman enough for
the job, but he was not so sure about his power of
getting through the country. He, therefore, one day,
quietly seated himself inside this man's coach, and
after a time his doubts were confirmed, for on pulling
up at a roadside inn, the landlady, without observing
him, said to the coachman, "Mr. So-and-So, how
will you have your eggs done to-day? Shall they
be poached or boiled?" I need hardly add, he remained on the slow coach.

A smart coachman usually took his place in
changing horses, and it is quite possible, as I know
from experience, having been timed by a box
passenger, to effect the change in one minute and a
half, with only one horse-keeper, assisted by coachman
and guard; but to do this, each one must know his

own place; they must not be tumbling over one another. The best drill I ever knew for this purpose was as follows: As the coach gradually stopped, the guard got down, and ran forward to unhook the near leader's outside trace, and then drew the near lead rein through the territs, after which he changed the near wheel horse, and finished by running the near lead rein. The horse-keeper, on the off-side, unhooked the remaining lead traces, uncoupled the wheel horses, and changed the off-side one. The coachman, getting down from his box as fast as he could, finished changing the leaders. The horses had, of course, previous to the arrival of the coach, been properly placed; one wheeler on each side of the road, and the leaders coupled.

This, of course, could only be carried out when the team was pretty quiet to " put to," for with queer tempered ones, all sorts of dodges had to be resorted to, attended sometimes with considerable loss of time.

Occasionally, it would be necessary to run a leader's rein the first thing, and then the coachman had to bustle up to his box as quick as he could, trusting to the horse-keeper and guard to get the traces hooked as best they might. Again, some wheelers could not bear to be poled up till after the coach was started. Horse-keepers were often exceedingly smart at this sort of work, though they varied a good deal, so much so, that it was no uncommon thing for "queer ones" to start better from one end of the stage than the other.

These said horse-keepers were a rough lot, and no great wonder, for they had rough work to do They were frequently expected to attend to eight horses, four out and four in, every day, or to take charge of six, with eight out and eight in, during the course of the day. But, what was worse than the work, they constantly had vicious horses to attend to, and such as it was dangerous to approach in the stall. To meet this difficulty, I have known a long cord used, with one end fastened to the head collar, and the other made fast to the stall-post, by which the horse could be pulled back far enough to enable the horse-keeper to keep clear of his heels whilst entering the stall. I was once travelling at night, when, upon arriving at the end of a stage, the coachman said to the horse-keeper, "Mind what you are about with that horse," pointing to a fresh one, "he bit a piece out of a man just before starting." It struck me as not a very enviable position to be left, in the middle of a dark night, to look single-handed after four dirty horses, and one of them a "savage."

But to return to changing horses, for it was an item of the very greatest importance in fast work. It was necessary at times to use a twitch with kickers, or to strap up one foreleg, though I have known this latter insufficient to keep the hind feet on the ground, and was once compelled to "Rarey" a mare before she would suffer herself to be put to the coach. She was, from some cause or another, the worst tempered horse I ever met with. When I first knew her, she was the property of a gentleman residing at Dolgelly, but her temper was so violent and untractable, that she had got the better of one or two breakers, and the ostler at the "Wynnstay Arms" at Machynlleth, having undertaken to conquer her, she had been taken there for that purpose.

It happened that I had promised to drive, a day or two afterwards, for another coachman, who wanted a rest, and as his coach did not start till after I had arrived with the "Harkaway" from Barmouth, and was back again in time for my return coach, I was able to oblige him, little thinking what I had undertaken.

On looking over the team before mounting my box, what should I espy but this very animal at off-lead. "Oh," says I, "then this is the way you are going to be broken? Well, we shall see how we can agree." And taking up the reins, I mounted the box. Cautioning the horse-keeper not to touch her, but to keep alongside the other leader through the archway out of the inn yard, and to be sure and make him carry his bar well, we started, the hitherto unmanageable mare giving very little trouble, and, after a few more journeys in the coach, she was considered to have finished her education, and returned home.

I suppose, however, that she was not much to the taste of her owner, as she was very soon purchased, for a small sum, by my partner, Mr. E. Jones, of the "Ship Hotel," Dolgelly, and put to run in the "Harkaway." I drove her for many months, and considered that she was quite subdued, though it was always necessary to strap up a foreleg when putting her to the coach, and she was always nasty in the stable. All of a sudden, however, as spring came on, she returned to her old tricks, and thought so little of having a leg strapped up, that she kicked her bar over the top of the coach, and was so violent that it was impossible to "put her to." I determined, therefore, to "Rarey" her, so, getting a long rope, and fastening it to the foreleg which was not strapped, and passing it over her withers, I gradually pulled her down, and, after the most approved "Rarey" fashion, sat upon her. After a few minutes, I allowed her to get up, but she seemed still to be very light behind, so I put her into her place at near-lead, all the while keeping a strain upon the rope, and so kept her peaceable whilst the traces were hooked, the rein run, etc. Then, handing over the rope to the guard, I got into my place, when it became, "Let 'em go, and take care of yourselves." The brute went right

CHAPTER XV.

GUARDS.

THE guard of the olden day was generally exceedingly quick in putting on the skid and taking it off, which with fast coaches travelling hilly roads, before the patent break was in use, was of first-rate importance. Most of them were able to do the former without entirely stopping the coach, but only a very few could unskid without the coachman pulling up and backing his horses. It required a man of unusual strength and activity to unskid whilst the coach was in motion, as it was necessary for him to twist the wheel back out of the pan with the right hand, and at the same moment to seize the chain with the left, and hang it to the hook on the coach, and these skid-pans were not a very light weight.

Probably few of my readers will know the manner in which wheels were dragged in a frost, therefore I will try and explain it here. It is manifest that the usual way of doing it would have been not only useless, but absolutely mischievous, as it would have had a tendency to pull the hind part of the coach into the side of the road when it was slippery. The method adopted, therefore, was to tie a strong chain round the felloe of the wheel, in such a position that it pressed upon the ground and broke up the surface sufficiently to get a good hold on it. This chain was then fastened to the safety hook.

Guards were frequently obliged to work very long hours, as it was usually the case that, on coaches running long distances, one of them would cover the ground driven over by four coachmen. In severe weather this was naturally very trying, consequently, they did not work every day. For instance, the "Wonder," from Shrewsbury to London, a distance of one hundred and fifty-four miles, had three guards, each of whom worked two double journeys and then rested for one. The object of these men going the whole journey no doubt was that there should be no break in the parcel department, which might have caused delay or loss.

Talking of the "Wonder" reminds me that, fast as it travelled, the proprietors had intended doing better. The late Mr. Taylor, who horsed it out of Shrewsbury, told me that it had been in contemplation to expedite it so as to perform the journey in thirteen hours instead of sixteen, and that, to enable this pace to be kept up, the stages would have been limited to six miles each, and the coach was not to stop to pick up passengers, or for any other business, except at

Everything had to be done at the "change," as there was no convenience for the guard to go over his parcels, as is done in a van on the railways. By the bye, I wonder what John Ash would have thought of himself if he had got down from the back of the "Wonder" with a pencil behind his ear?

To a certain extent, what were termed "shorts" were allowed, as it was customary for all passengers' fares not exceeding two shillings to be the perquisite of the coachman and guard on coaches, and of the latter only on mails, as he was the servant of the proprietors, carrying the way-bill and having charge of the parcels. The Post-office guard was occupied with his bags; but his was a rather anomalous position, receiving only the munificent sum of ten shillings and sixpence a week from the Post Office, and being supposed to eke out a living by fees from the passengers, to whom he had little or no time to attend. Of quite late years, however, this was corrected, and the few who were then employed were more liberally dealt with. They received as much as seventy pounds a year from the Post Office; but then they were not supposed to take fees from the passengers, or, at any rate, not to ask for them. So much was this system of "shorts" an acknowledged thing, that I have had two shillings handed to me by the book-keeper as I was getting on to my box, with the following remark, "I took it from him, thinking he might fork out something more when he gets down." These perquisites, however, were not altogether untaxed, as coachmen were expected to subsidize the wages of the horse-keepers to the amount of one shilling a week, and sometimes more.

Talking of parcels brings to my mind a rather comical scene I once witnessed. It so happened that one day I came across one of the "Tourist" coaches, running between Caernarvon and Dolgelly, which had pulled up at a wayside inn about thirteen miles from Tan-y-bwlch. I was attracted by the coach-man, whose name was, if I recollect rightly, Roberts, intently studying the address on a small parcel. It evidently caused him great trouble to decipher it, as he first turned it up, and then he turned it down, but neither right side up nor wrong side up could he satisfy himself, and, at last, looking up and seeing me, he came for assistance out of his difficulties, saying he was not a very good scholar. When I looked at the address, I said, "You should have left this at Tan-y-bwlch." "Well, dear me," said he, "that was a bad job; indeed, it is doctor's stuff."

CHAPTER XVI.

WHERE DID THEY ALL GO TO ?

HAVING indicated to some extent the sources from which the great demand for coachmen were supplied, I will venture to dwell, for a moment, and not without feelings of regret, on the subject of their no less rapid disappearance from the scene. It will, I am aware, have little or no interest to many : well, then, let them skip it ; but some there may be, into whose hands this little volume finds its way, who have sufficient remembrance of old days to be interested in it, and, at any rate, it shall not occupy much space.

It is always a melancholy thing to see any class of men suddenly deprived of their means of subsistence from no fault of their own. It is very easy to say that if one trade fails another must be found, and to some political economists this appears to be a sufficient solution of the difficulty, but it by no means has that effect on the sufferers. A man who has thoroughly learned one handicraft, can very seldom become a proficient in any others ; and it is always the inferior workmen who are left out in the cold. Driving, like

other trades, was not learned without much practice,
and does not fit a man for any other business.
Where, then, did they vanish to ?

The guards could, and I believe did, to a large
extent, find employment on the railways in the same
capacity, and, probably, some coachmen also; but this
could not absorb all, or, indeed, any very large proportion of them.   His means of subsistence consisted
in his power of driving horses.   He could not drive
a steam engine.   It is difficult to say where they all
dispersed to.   A considerable number, no doubt, found
employment upon omnibuses in London and other
large towns; but that was a sorry life, indeed, like
slavery compared to freedom, to one who had been
accustomed to the cheery work on a coach.

Many of those who had had the good fortune to
drive good paying coaches, and had been thrifty,
invested their savings in inns, and, in some cases, in
hotels of some importance.   A few, some of whom I
have previously mentioned, followed the receding tide,
and obtained drives upon summer coaches.   One who
could horse a stage was pretty sure of getting a drive
on one of them, as there was frequently some diffi
culty in finding people to cover the middle ground.
Some few took to farming, but I cannot call to mind
anyone who prospered as an agriculturist.

I fear the larger part died off rapidly.   They were
never a long-lived class of men.   Strange as it may

sound, the natural healthiness of the employment tended to shorten their lives. The constant passing through the air promoted great appetites, which, for the most part were fully gratified, and this, together with insufficient exercise, produced disease. I have known some who took a good walk before or after the day's drive, who lived to a hale old age, but too many seemed to think that the driving was sufficient exercise, though it could only have been very bad teams that made it so; worse than were put to coaches of late years.

Joe Wall, who drove the Manchester " Telegraph " out of London, used to take his exercise in a very aristocratic manner, as he always kept one, and sometimes two hunters, at Hockliffe, where he left the coach, and enjoyed his love for sport, as well as getting healthy exercise, and occupying the time which would otherwise have hung heavy on his hands, and possibly might have led him into mischief. This, however, had its drawbacks, and, on one occasion, was very near leading to a difficulty of no small magnitude. He had, as usual, been out hunting, and had, unfortunately, experienced a bad fall, which incapacitated him from driving the return coach, and, at first, it seemed as if it could not find its way to London that evening, for it was not every one, even though he might call himself a coachman, who was capable of driving a coach at the pace at which the " Telegraph " was timed, on a dark winter's evening, along a road crowded with so large a number of vehicles of all descriptions as would be the case on one approaching the metropolis. As good luck, however, would have it, an efficient substitute turned up in the shape of a very able and experienced hand, who had driven equally fast coaches. A few became horse-dealers, and I knew one who was for many years the highly-valued stud-groom to the late Sir W. W. Wynn, but, if I ever heard it, I have quite forgotten what coach it was that Simpson drove. I believe he was a good coachman, but he had the misfortune, though by no fault of his own, to capsize the hound van, nearly killing that prince of huntsmen, John Walker.

I once knew a guard who had previously followed the occupation of clown in a circus. His experience there had made him active enough for anything, but he and the coachman did not, I fancy, get on very well together, as the latter used sometimes to speak of him in derision as " my fool."

CHAPTER XVII.

SOME CHARACTERS.

THERE was a great character who drove out of Machynlleth at that time. His name was David Lloyd, and he worked the mail between that place and Dolgelly round by Towyn and the coast. When he came to a certain long fall of ground, he would put his team into a gallop, and then, taking a small twisted horn, which he slung in a strap over his shoulder, would blow almost without ceasing, especially when it was dusk, as was more or less the case during a considerable part of the year, and, as his right hand was fully occupied with the horn, if he wanted to take a pull at the reins he made use of his foot.

It was dark for the greater part of the year before he reached the end of the journey, and, as his sight was not very good at night, he would sometimes say to his box passenger, " If you please, sir, will you tell me what is coming towards us." Perhaps the passenger, after looking, would say "A cart," to which David would reply, " Then I was get out of his way ; " but if the answer was "A gig," or "A carriage," he would say, " Then he was get out of my way," and would keep straight on.

Dolgelly at that time contained a few boon companions, some of whom were rather given to practical joking. One morning there happened to be on the box seat one of these gentlemen, and when they had proceeded a few miles on the road, he pulled a pill-box out of his pocket and took some of the pills. Upon seeing this, David said to him, " If you please, sir, what have you got there ? " He replied, " Only a few pills, which I find very beneficial after a hard night." " Well, indeed," says David, " I had a rather heavy night; was you please give me some of them ? " " All right," says he, " hold out your hand," when he poured several pills into it ; and upon David asking how many he was to take, he said, " Take them all," which he did ; and the sequel was, that he drove his coach to Machynlleth, but another man brought it back in the evening.

For two summers, when I was driving the Aberystwith and Kington " Cambrian," I had Ben Haslam as guard, who was also something of a character, and quite one of the old coachmen. He had driven for many years out of London on different coaches, and, like a good many others, had followed the receding tide, and had got down to Herefordshire, where coaches lingered for several years, and then on to Wales, where, at that time, railways had not penetrated.

He was full of anecdotes connected with the road, and towards autumn, when the down loads were usually very light, I would sometimes get him to sit by me on the box that he might enliven the way with some of them.

He had one story which amused me, of the only really crusty coachman I ever heard of. They were, as a rule, very cheery, genial spirits, and, indeed, had not much cause to be otherwise. There were few pleasanter lives. They were generally made a great deal of, indeed, perhaps rather too much so at times, although, as a body, they bore their honours becomingly. Between the patronage they received from the gentlemen and the deference shown them by the horse-keepers and others, it is hardly to be wondered at if sometimes their heads were a little turned, and they became rather too big for their boots. There was a story told of one, who was rather cheeky, giving great offence to a parson, who was his box passenger, by saying that he was not going to drive the next day, but should send his curate. They were, however, not very unfrequently taken down a peg by a lick from the rough side of a crusty proprietor's tongue ; but on the whole, they were, as Tony Weller said, "priviledged indiwiduals."

But to return to the crusty coachman. His name was Spooner, and he drove out of Oxford, and, though often causing trouble with the passengers by his want

of urbanity, he was too valuable a servant to get rid
of. As was not so very unusual with him, he had
been lately called to account for some want of civility
to a passenger, whereupon he announced his deter-
mination never to speak to one of them again, and
he kept his word, till one day, a gentleman who was
going to travel by his coach, asked him some question,
but after repeating it several times and eliciting no
reply, turned to the proprietor, who was in the office,
saying, " Your coachman is so surly, he won't answer
a single question I put to him." The proprietor asked
him what he meant by not answering the gentleman,
to which he replied, " If I do speak to him he will
only complain, like that other fool did the other day."

On another occasion his whole coach was occupied
by musicians, coming to play at a ball at Oxford,
and, as he did not expect very good pay from them,
he was not in the best of tempers. It happened that
at the last change of horses before arriving at Oxford,
a boy, who had been sent with a fresh horse, was
returning by the coach, and, as every seat was occu
pied, he sat upon the footboard by the bandmaster's
feet, and after they had gone a short distance, pulled
a Jew's harp out of his pocket and began to play
upon it. Upon this the bandmaster asked the boy
to allow him to try what he could do with it, saying,
" He could play a good many instruments, but had
never tried a Jew's harp." The new instrument proved

too much for him, whereupon old Spooner looked at him with scorn and contempt, and said, " You are a pretty sort of a man for a bandmaster, and cannot play a Jew's harp."

He also narrated how, when the Great Western Railway was opened over only certain lengths, and coaches were employed over the other ground, some of those were conveyed certain distances on trucks, and the coachmen travelled in their respective coaches. Of course they did not overflow with affection for their rivals, and the way they tried to annoy them was by getting out of their coaches and applying the breaks to the wheels of the trucks.

This reminds me of how very slow all those connected with coaches, as also those who took a warm interest in them, were to realize the fact that their occupation was fast leaving them, and that the railways would, before many years, have entirely superseded the old system of travelling.

We were not, however, the only people who were somewhat sceptical on the subject, though with us, no doubt, the wish was father to the thought; but the *Times* newspaper, whilst admitting the financial success of the Liverpool and Manchester Railway, warned investors against speculative imitation, saying, " Where there are good roads and convenient coaches, it would be a mistake to alter existing arrangements."

Every little failure of the railways raised our

spirits and gave strength to the hope that they would fail, as all attempts to utilize steam upon ordinary roads had hitherto done. At first, they were unable to keep time in frosty weather, as the driving-wheels kept turning round and round on the same spot of the slippery rail.

In the beginning of January, in the year 1838, I was travelling down to Shrewsbury by the Holyhead mail. It was the first night of the long frost and snow-up of that winter, which continued for two months, and the roads were so much blocked up with snow, that for a few days the coachmen and guards held a sort of wake at Dunchurch. On the night I travelled down the frost set in exceedingly sharp, and the only up mail that kept time was the Holyhead, which had come by road the whole distance through North Wales. The other mails, whose bags had been brought to Birmingham by what was then called the Grand Junction Railway, were after time, as the trains could make but slow progress on the slippery rails. The coachman and I, two silly creatures as we were, made ourselves happy with the conviction that railways must always be a failure for fast work, and that the coaching business was not in such great danger after all. No doubt this opinion was entertained by a good many others, and led to losses, by inducing some coach proprietors to oppose the railways instead of coming to terms with them.

It was on this journey, if I recollect rightly, that I had my last experience of that conveyance, long since quite lost to sight, and now nearly so to memory, that perhaps I may be pardoned if I linger for a few moments to raise it, or its ghost, before the eyes of the present generation, especially as I have seen some not very accurate descriptions of them.

The old hackney coach, though frousty and damp, was generally roomy and easy, as it had nearly always commenced its career in gentlemen's service, and had consequently been built by one of the best coachmakers of the day, and so far was decidedly better than the modern "bounder." It carried about it a character of decayed respectability, not to say grandeur, and upon entering one of them it was not impossible for a gentleman to be greeted by his own quarterings upon the panel. They were as ramshackling looking things as could be imagined, with, occasionally, wheels of different colours, and the horses and coachman, together with his clothes, seemed made to match.

But to return to coaches proper again: one called the "Dart" used to run between Oxford and London, driven by a coachman who was commonly known by the name of "Black Will;" and one fine morning the box seat was occupied by an Oxford Don, who thought he would enjoy the air on his journey. After they had gone a short distance he addressed our friend Black Will, saying, "Are you the coachman they call Black Will?" His answer was, "Blackguards call me Black Will, but gentlemen call me Mr. Walters." It is needless to say that this shut up the Don for the remainder of the journey.

Dick Dicas drove the "Cambrian" between Llangollen and Dolgelly for several years, and one day it so happened that among the outside passengers there was a ventriloquist. As they drove along the road a man was seen walking leisurely across a field in the direction of the coach, when the ventriloquist threw his voice so as to make it appear that he was calling to it to stop. Of course, Dick pulled up, thinking he had got another passenger; but as he did not quicken his pace, he began to get impatient, for he was not a Job under any circumstances, and called out to him to "Come on," and "Do you suppose I can wait here all day for you?" At last, as he approached nearer, he said, "What do you want with me?" when friend Dick answered, "Why, you called me to stop." "I did nothing of the sort," replied the man in the field. "I tell you you did," said Dick, waxing warmer. "Well, I'm not coming with you, anyhow," said the leisurely man; whereupon there was nothing left for Dick to do but to drive on, not in the best of tempers, as may be supposed. Whether he ever knew of the trick played upon him I do not remember to have heard, but if he did find it out in time, I suspect he made it hot for the ventriloquist.

At one time Cambridge could boast of a clever poet as a coachman.   Tom Cross was his name, and he drove the Lynn coach from the "Golden Cross," Charing Cross.   He wrote "The Conflagration of Rome," and "Paul before Nero," and some wags among the undergraduates said the idea was given him by the fat from the bacon he was frying in the garret igniting.   But be that as it may, they were very clever compositions.   I fancy it was this man who published the first book on coaching which has appeared in print.

CHAPTER XVIII.

MONOTONY.

I HAVE sometimes been asked if I did not find it very monotonous to be always travelling the same road day after day. Some might have found it so, but I never did. There was never wanting something to break through the monotony. One was brought into contact with fresh passengers every journey, and constantly some fresh incident arose. Indeed, on many roads the scenery alone would beguile the time. In leafy England there are few roads on which there is not something to admire, even if other parts are devoid of attraction, and with the real lover of scenery, the eye does not easily tire of looking at the same picture. I must admit that I have been especially favoured in this respect, as my drives lay through some of the most lovely scenery in Wales, notably the valley of the Mawddach, so eulogistically spoken of by the late Judge Talfourd ; and also the magnificent scenery of Snowdonia. I can never forget the remarkable reflection in the water with which I was once favoured at Port

Madoc, on the down journey from Caernarvon to Aberystwith. As we passed over the embankment and bridge, which at that place unite the counties of Caernarvon and Merioneth, the whole of the mountain range for many miles round, including Snowdon and the remarkable peak-shaped Cnicht, together with many other mountains, whose names I cannot now call to mind, were reflected in the clear water of the estuary, which was then at full tide, as clearly as they could have been in a mirror. It was a sight not to be erased from memory.

Then, again, he was a fortunate man who drove seventy or eighty miles a day, who had no horse to deal with which would not pretty effectually banish *ennui* for one stage. Again, the coach was the bringer of the news of the day, and, moreover, never stayed long enough in one place but that it was always "welcome in and welcome out," and this brings to my mind a rather amusing incident—at least, it was good fun to one side—which occurred at a contested election a good many years ago.

On the occasion of a warmly-contested election for Montgomeryshire, in the year 1862, I had been to Welshpool to vote for my friend Mr. C. W. W. Wynn, and when, on my down journey, I arrived at Machynlleth, there being no electric telegraph, great anxiety was felt to know the state of the poll. This I gave them as far as it was known when I left Welshpool, but the returns from some of the strongest Conservative districts not having then been received, it was very far from perfection. However, it being favourable to the other side, they jumped at it, and it was not my business to undeceive them ; so in their flush of confidence and the height of their happiness, they backed their man freely. The next morning, when I returned with my up coach, the final result of the poll was known, which was in favour of the Conservatives, and they had only to pay and look pleased, which, to their credit, I believe they did very good-humouredly.

I think I have now shown that if there is monotony in always driving the same road, it may, at any rate, be monotony with variations, and a strong opposition at once scattered it all to the winds, as one day one would be in front, and on another the other one.

Night driving had always a strong fascination for me. The sensation of always, as it were, driving into darkness, not knowing what would appear next, kept up the zest of the thing. I do not mean to say that I was in love with poking along in a dark night with only two indifferent lamps ; but having time to keep, and plenty of light, I did enjoy. No fast coach could be said to be efficiently lighted without five lamps—two on each side and one under the foot-board. The best lamps for throwing a strong light

forward which I ever used, were made by Messrs.
Kay and Johnson, of Edinburgh. They were what
were designated "Argand burners," and being constructed strong and without unnecessary ornament,
were sold to stage coachmen for four pounds ten
shillings the pair. As they only threw their light
nearly straight ahead, they required to be supplemented, except upon very wide, good roads, by
other lamps placed lower down on the coach, which
threw a strong light to the side; and with them, and
one under the footboard, if there were no fog, the
darkest night could be set at defiance. I always
used the best sperm oil, as I found that colza oil had
a tendency to become thick from the shaking of the
coach, which caused the brightness of the light to
become dimmed.

At night, also, a coachman must depend upon his
hands to tell him how his horses are working, and as
he may never see some of the teams by daylight at
all, his left hand is all he has got to rely upon to
inform him how the horse-keepers are doing their
duty by the stock, and whether they are doing well
or not.

CHAPTER XIX.

TANDEM.

I HAVE never been very much of a tandem driver, for having been entered upon stage coaches, and driven them for a good many hundred miles before getting hold of a tandem, I must confess I rather looked down upon it, and regarded it somewhat in the light of a toy.

The first time of my embarking in one I felt like the proverbial tin kettle to the dog's tail. There was no weight behind the horses to bring them to their collars, and they appeared to be almost drawing by my hands, like the Yankee trotters. Of course, that sensation went off after a little practice, and, though it is a team that requires careful handling, it is one exceedingly well adapted for heavy roads, as there is great strength of horse power in proportion to the load which is usually placed behind them. This not only enables one to ascend steep hills with ease, but also greatly facilitates the descent, as it is almost impossible to place a sufficient load upon only two wheels to overpower the shaft horse. It was in the

act of descending hills that most coach accidents
happened, by the load overpowering the wheel
horses ; and, of course, the load on a tandem cart can
never be top heavy, which was another fertile source
of accidents to coaches.

When I first tried my hand at tandem I was
quartered at Chatham, and being cut off from the
coaches I had been accustomed to drive, my hands
itched for the double reins, and I condescended to the
hitherto despised tandem ; but upon my first attempt,
I soon found myself brought up with the leader on
one side a small tree and the wheeler on the other.
Rather a humiliating position for one who thought
himself a coachman ! At that time, however, I little
realized how much practice is required to master the
science of driving, though I must confess that something short of that ought to have kept me clear of
the tree.

This brings to my recollection a scene which
occurred during the time I was quartered in that
garrison, which throws some light on the manners
and customs of military life half a century ago.

It so happened, as also occurred to Mr. Pickwick
and his friends on another occasion, that a ball was
held at the Assembly Rooms in Rochester, and a
good sprinkling of officers from the barracks were
present, among which I counted one. When the
small hours of the morning were reached, and it was

time to return home, another officer and I, each in
full uniform, jumped on the boxes of two of what
were then termed "dicky chaises," and raced nearly
as fast as the old screws could gallop along the streets
of Rochester and Chatham up to the barracks; and
upon our arriving there the gates were thrown open,
and we did not finish our race till we reached the
officers' quarters.

It was, however, in the Australian colonies that I
did most of my tandem driving, and as the roads in
those new countries were often, to say the least of
it, imperfectly made, and houses were few and far
between, causing a journey of sixty or seventy miles
in the day to be sometimes necessary, I found it a
team by no means to be despised.

It was early in the year of 1840 that I landed at
Hobart Town (now abbreviated to Hobart), from the
good ship "Layton," of five hundred tons burden, after
a voyage of nearly five months, which had brought out
four hundred convicts, who were in those days sent out
under a small military guard; and it was not long after
finding myself on terra firma before the old craving
took possession of me, nor long after that before it was
gratified, as already a good foundation had been laid.

A dear old brother officer, many years dead, who
had gone out with a previous guard, had had a
tandem cart built; and he also supplied leader and
harness, I finding wheeler and coachman, as he did not

care for driving; so I think I had the best of it. However, both were satisfied, which is not always the case.

In that lovely island, then called Van Diemen's Land, but now Tasmania, there were many miles of roads as good as any to be found in England, constructed by convict labour, and admirably engineered over the hills. Indeed, the greater part of the one hundred and twenty miles between Hobart and Launceston was good enough for almost any pace, as I can vouch for from having driven the whole distance both ways.

I was not, however, allowed to remain in that delightful island for long, but was sent away with a detachment of two companies to the colony then called Swan River, but now changed to West Australia; and there we bid adieu to roads such as are generally understood by that word. All that was ever done there at that time was to cut off the trees, when they were in great numbers, about a foot from the ground; so anyone may imagine how the horses stumbled over one stump and the wheels bounded over another. In other places, where the trees were few and the bush thin, nothing was done unless it were what was called "blazing," which consisted of cutting off a piece of bark from some of the trees to indicate what was meant to be a road; but in many parts nothing at all had been done, and the traveller had nothing to show him the road except a few wheel

marks, and was obliged to thread his way between the
trees as best he could. Even in the settlements there
was no attempt at macadam.

These were just the circumstances to show off a
tandem to the best advantage and for finding out its
merits, which I soon had an opportunity of doing, as
an agricultural gathering was to be held at a place
called York, about eighty miles from the capital,
Perth, where we were quartered.

My old friend and I determined to make a start
for the scene of festivity. The tandem cart, which
had come with us, was looked over, and the harness
rubbed up; but the difficulty was how to get horsed,
as we had none of our own at that time. However,
without very much trouble we engaged two of some
sort, though one of them turned out to be as much
plague as profit, as the sequel will show. He was in
the lead, and for a good while we were quite unable to
make him budge an inch in the right direction. At
last we saddled him, and my companion mounting,
armed with a good stick, began to lay about him so
vigorously that the brute made off fast enough; but
his rider was so intent on keeping him moving that he
quite forgot to look what direction he was going in,
and led the way off the road into the bush, though,
indeed, there was little difference between them. I
was almost falling off my box from laughter, much
less was I able to make myself heard to recall him

into the road.   At last, however, the direction was
changed and the road regained, but I don't think I
have ever laughed so much before or since, so
ridiculous was the scene.

Well, we managed to get as far as the first
settlement on the road, about ten miles, where a good
many others, all riding, had collected from different
parts, and were bound to the same destination ; and
here we met with a Good Samaritan indeed, in the
shape of a friend who had settled in the colony, and
was riding a very nice quiet mare, which he most
kindly exchanged with us for our leader.   The only
drawback to this arrangement was that she was
followed by a foal at her heels, which every now and
then would pass between the leader and wheeler, and
it was as much as I could do to avoid injuring it.

We travelled pretty comfortably, however, in this
manner for a good many miles till it became dark,
when it was necessary to light the lamps, as there
remained some miles to be covered before arriving at
the end of the day's journey ; the delay at starting
having thrown us behind time.

If it was difficult to thread the way among the
stumps and avoid running over the foal in the
daylight, I leave the reader to judge what it was after
dark ; sufficient to say that we jumped and bumped
first over one stump and then over another, the
horses continually blundering over them as well.

However, all's well that ends well, and we reached the journey's end at last for that day. A solitary hostelry it was in the midst of the bush, miles distant from any other habitation, generally little used, but on the present occasion full to overflowing. As we approached the house in the dark, voices as of quarrelling reached our ears, for it so happened that a certain naval officer, who was not usually given to falling out, but who, like many others of his craft, was safer "aloft" than on a horse's back, had just ridden up at a sharp pace to the house, and the landlord, appearing at the door with a light at the same moment, made the horse stop short, which caused the rider to be deposited on the ground, and he, thinking it had been done intentionally, was very wrathful ; mine host, also becoming heated, made use of the words that had caught my ears as I drove up, which were, " If the gentleman wants a game of fives, I am his man." After a few minutes, however, peace-makers appeared upon the scene, explanations took place, and harmony was restored.

The house was so crowded that none but those who had taken the precaution to bespeak beds before-hand could get them, and, of those, I will not venture to say how many slept in the same one. The rest of us had to deposit our carcases where we could, and I got possession of a sofa, in what I suppose must be called the coffee-room, where I lay down and went to sleep, but only for a very short time, as the bugs, the most voracious I ever met with, nearly pulled me off it. I then tried the floor, but with, if possible, worse results, so, like the man in the song of the "Cork Leg," "I soon got up and was off again."

By this time I had had enough of the inside of the house, and therefore betook myself out of it, where I found some natives in their small tents made of bark, and gathering some wood and getting a light from them, I soon had a fire, and lying down by it, with the driving cushion for a pillow, passed the rest of the night in peace and comfort. Probably by this time a railway has been constructed through this country, and for all I know a grand company hotel may have taken the place of the old "Half-way House" in the bush.

These said natives always went about in those days, and probably do now—though perhaps civilization and Bryant and May may have rendered it unnecessary—well provided with a light; and it was the usual thing, when meeting them in the bush, to see one or two women carrying what was termed a fire stick, which consisted of two pieces of bark placed together, and of such a nature that it kept alight for a considerable length of time; nor, indeed, to anyone who had witnessed the labour it was to them to strike a light in their primitive fashion, would this carefulness of the household fire excite any wonder. I will endeavour to explain how they did it.

As was my frequent custom, I was passing a few days in the bush, hunting kangaroos, and the first evening upon arriving at our camping ground, we told the native, who was accompanying us as guide, that he must strike a light, but he replied, " No, white fellow make fire." We said, " Black fellow have no fire to-night if he no make it ; " and after a good deal of persuasion he was prevailed upon to set to work, which he did in the following manner :—

First, he cut a sort of reed which grew upon a shrub, which went by the name of the black boy, bringing one end to a point. He then got a flat piece of stick, about a foot in length, in the middle of which he made a small hole, just large enough to hold the pointed end of the reed. Then after heaping a small quantity of the dryest old leaves he could find upon the flat stick, he inserted the point of the reed into the hole in it in an upright position, then holding the stick firm by sitting down and putting his feet upon it, he commenced to rub the reed backwards and forwards between his hands so energetically that in the space of about ten minutes or less, some smoke made its appearance, which was very soon followed by fire. It was certainly an ingenious way of striking a light, but decidedly laborious, and very primitive even in comparison with the old tinder-box and matches, which

I can recollect as the only means the *civilized* world had of obtaining a light.

Like other savages living in fine climates, where food could be obtained with little labour, they were naturally indolent, of which I had an amusing instance on one occasion.

I was walking one very hot summer day along what, by courtesy, was called a street in Perth, which—though laid out with the view of being at some future time, and now probably is, a wide and handsome thoroughfare—consisted at that time of deep sand, when, from a native sitting basking in the sunshine on the opposite side, I was accosted in a plaintive tone with the words, " White fellow, money give it 'em." I pulled some small coin out of my pocket, and held it out in my hand for him to fetch, but instead of exerting himself to get up, he said, " Oh, white fellow bring it 'em." After this length of time I cannot charge my memory with what the result was, but suppose he had to fetch it.

It is much to the credit of the settlers in this colony that these children of nature had, at that time, and I dare say it is the same now, been always kindly treated, and so far from the advent of the white man being the signal for the diminution of the dusky one, the Aborigines, in some parts of the colony at the time I am speaking of, were actually increasing in numbers. Especially was this the case with the tribe which lived round Perth, and it was accounted for in this way.

They had a rough and ready way of maintaining the balance of power among themselves, which was that upon the death of a man in one tribe, one of his relations speared one belonging to some other adjoining tribe to keep the balance even, and as what was called the Perth tribe was supposed to be under the protection of the whites, they were left pretty much unmolested in this way.

Though averse to anything like labour, some of them made fairly good shepherds, but the same man was not allowed by his tribe to work continuously. I heard of a case in which one man regularly served a settler in the capacity of shepherd for six months in the year; that is to say, he worked for three months, after which he went away for the same length of time, sending another to fill his place; at the expiration of which time he returned to his charge for another three months. If he had taken service permanently, his tribe would have speared him, so jealous were they of their liberty, and, like many others better instructed, rejecting the good things within their reach.

I have made a long digression, which I hope has not wearied the reader, and it is time to return to the solitary hostelry in the bush, which was the only one at that time where any accommodation could be obtained for the whole journey between Perth and York.

At an early hour of the morning all the guests at the " Half-way House " were astir, comparing notes of their nocturnal experiences, and getting breakfast ; and when in due time a start was effected, there was a goodly cavalcade, we two being the only ones on wheels. Riding is the universal mode of traversing the bush.

At the " Half-way House " we had met with the man from whom we had hired our horses, and he changed with us, giving us the one he was riding, so that we were enabled to return the mare and foal to our kind benefactor, and we reached our destination the same day without any further adventures.

We had been kindly asked to stay at the house of a settler close to the settlement for two or three days, and he received us with that true and genuine hospitality which so universally distinguished the residents in all parts of Australia, and nowhere more than in the colony I am now writing about. Of course, the accommodation they could offer was not particularly commodious, but the welcome was warm, and nothing that could be obtained, and no trouble that could be taken, were considered too much to make the guests comfortable.

Though accommodation was always made in the

house for the guests, there were sometimes no stables, and the horses were obliged to be tethered in the bush near the house, and, consequently, no one ever thought of going from home without having a tether rope coiled round his horse's neck. Of course, in so sparsely populated a district, houses were few and far between, and, consequently, there was but little society, though a matter of twenty miles or so would not deter one resident from visiting another ; and as news was scarce in these backwoods, anyone coming from the more accessible parts, and therefore a bearer of news, especially if it emanated from the " Old Country," was very acceptable.

As I remarked before, however, occasionally, at the less busy times of the year, one settler would ride over to pay a visit to a neighbour fifteen or twenty miles distant, and having arrived at his destination, after removing the saddle and bridle, and tethering his horse, would offer himself at the house, where he was certain of finding a hearty welcome.

There was a story told of one having done this who, after enjoying himself till well on in the night, and having been rather powerfully refreshed, thinking it time to return home, replaced the saddle and bridle upon his horse, but forgot all about the tether rope, and, consequently, continued riding round and round in a circle, whilst he most complacently thought he was pursuing his homeward journey.

After partaking of our good friend's hospitality for two or three days, we retraced our steps to Perth, without anything occurring worthy of note ; but fully convinced, by experience, of the peculiar adaptability of tandem for travelling over bush roads. It would hardly be possible to use a four-wheel carriage under such circumstances.

In those out-of-the-way places people cannot be very particular, and are obliged to improvise things as best they can. On one occasion, when visiting a friend in the bush, I came across two others, who were driving an unusual team. I can only designate it as an " inverted pick-axe." It consisted of a horse, as usual, in the shafts of a dog-cart, with two abreast in front of him. Upon remarking on the peculiarity of the turn-out, and asking how it answered, I was told that the team was not very handy. The cause of this did not require much time to discover, for there were no coupling reins to the leaders, who were only kept together, like G O horses in a plough, by a single strap. With the help of some strong string I rigged out coupling reins, and they went on their way rejoicing.

The danger commonly alleged against tandem is that the leader can turn round and face you. I never had this happen to me, but fancy it is little to be dreaded if the coachman will not loose his thong, but keep it caught up ready to administer a good dose of double thong over the horse's face as soon as he comes within reach. If worst comes to worst, however, a two-wheeled conveyance is able to turn on its own ground, and follow the horses, even if it is in the wrong direction.

CHAPTER XX.

THE CONVICT SHIP.

In the last chapter the reader was casually introduced to a convict ship, and as it is now about half a century since they became obsolete, it may not be altogether without interest to some readers to have a short account of them from one who can say *quorum pars fui.* I will therefore venture upon a short digression, which, though it introduces a subject foreign to the one which this little book professes to treat upon, nevertheless may yet bring a coach upon the stage when least expected.

Probably to the mind of some readers the very name of a convict ship will conjure up all sorts of horrors, culminating in a surprise, the capture of the ship by the convicts, and in all who resisted them being thrown overboard.

Well, at any rate, no such thing occurred on board the " Layton," nor did it ever on board any vessel carrying male convicts; though I have heard that such a thing did happen once to one conveying women, which having no military guard on board, the crew intrigued with the prisoners and carried the ship into some port on the South American coast.

The convicts were under the immediate charge of a naval surgeon, and, as I have already mentioned in the last chapter, he was supported by a small military guard. When first brought on board every man had irons on his legs, but upon the ship getting to sea, these were gradually knocked off as the surgeon considered could be done with safety.

One-third of the guard were always on duty on the poop of the ship, with their muskets (it was in the time of old "Brown Bess," with flint locks) loaded, and placed in a rack ready to hand; and to prevent any sudden rush to attack them, a strong wooden barricade was erected just abaft the mainmast, about seven feet high, with no opening through it except a small, low door in each gangway, just large enough to admit of one person passing through in a stooping posture.

With very few exceptions, the convicts gave no trouble. They had a saying among themselves that they were patriots, who left their country for their country's good; and an opportunity occurred during the voyage for some of them to do good service, which greatly improved their condition upon landing.

As is not very unfrequently the case in that latitude, when off the Cape de Verd Islands, the ship was caught in a violent squall, when the chief mate, who was in charge of the deck, "luffed up," and had commenced to take in sail, till the skipper appeared on the scene, who, without giving himself sufficient time to consider, immediately put the ship before the wind. By this action the sails, which were being reefed, were refilled suddenly, with the result of several of the masts and spars being carried away; and the saddest thing was that several of the crew, who were aloft at the time, went overboard with the rigging, and three poor fellows were drowned, notwithstanding all that could be done to save them.

I believe sailors recognize two ways of acting under these circumstances: the one what the mate did, to reduce sail; the other what the captain did, to run before the wind. As a land-lubber, I give no opinion between them; but a mixture of the two cannot help being fatal, as was the case with us. Never shall I forget the crash, crash, crash, of the falling masts. If, however, the skipper made a mistake this time, he showed himself quite equal to the occasion at a subsequent period of the voyage.

He and I were pacing the poop together, when suddenly the cabin-boy came up and whispered something to him which I did not catch, but which had the effect of making him scuttle at double-quick time. In about a quarter of an hour he returned, saying, "What do you think I was wanted for?" Of course, I answered, "I do not know." "Why," he replied, "they had set fire to a cask of spirits in the lazaret." "What on earth did you do?" I said. "Well," says he, "I sat upon the bunghole." This move on his part had the effect of excluding the air, and, consequently, of extinguishing the fire. It was a quick, smart thing to do, and saved what would have been an awful catastrophe—a ship on fire at sea, with about five hundred souls on board, and not boat accommodation enough for one hundred.

At the end of nearly a five months' voyage we found ourselves sailing up the beautiful Storm Bay, and never did land appear so lovely to my eyes before. The anchor was soon let down in the river Derwent, and the convict ship lay with her living freight off Hobart Town.

It is wonderful how time passes on board ship where there is nothing to mark it, and in this case the only break we had to the daily routine was occasional tiffs between the surgeon and the skipper. The former was anxious to get to the end of the voyage as quickly as possible, as he received ten shillings a head for all the prisoners that landed alive, and was sorely put out when every effort was not made to keep the old tub moving. The skipper, on the other hand, being paid by the month, preferred his comfort, and was fond of making all snug for the night in rough weather, and turning in, whilst we soldiers looked on with patience, if not contentment, for, as was the usual custom, we had received an advance of four months' pay upon leaving England, and didn't much care about landing till some more had become due. It is poor fun to go on shore with an empty pocket.

I believe it was unfortunate for the convicts that the system of transportation was obliged to be abandoned, as any of them in those new countries were able to return to an honest life if they really chose to do so, which, in an old and thickly populated country like England, is a very difficult thing to do. At the time I am writing about, the system of assigned servants was in practice, and though it was liable to much abuse, and was largely abused, still it had this advantage, that it admitted of their return to ordinary life long before their sentences had expired.

The system though, as I think, good in itself was shamefully administered, especially in the earliest years of the colony. At that time any free man or woman who had settled in the colony was not only entitled to a convict servant or servants, but could have any prisoner they liked, and this naturally led to the grossest abuses, of which the following is an example :—

Some men in England managed to find out that on a certain night, one of the mail coaches (and here comes in the coach) was to carry a large amount of bullion, which they concluded would be placed in the front boot of the coach, as the safest place, and in this they were not disappointed. They then secured the four inside places for that night, and whilst on the journey set to work to make a way into the boot and abstract the coin. Upon arriving at the end of the journey they immediately handed this over to their wives, who were in readiness to receive it, and straightway made off with it. The men were taken up, tried and convicted of the robbery, and sentenced to transportation. Soon after they landed in the new country they were assigned to their respective wives as servants, and, as is said in the children's story books, "lived very happily ever after."

Such a glaring case as this of course could hardly occur a second time, but sufficient care was never taken to see that convicts were only assigned to those masters whose character and position warranted it. At last, like many other things, good in themselves, it was abandoned altogether, instead of the trouble being taken to administer it properly.

There was one institution I must mention connected with convict life, as I suppose it was quite peculiar to Van Diemen's Land. A penal settlement was established for those who committed offences after their arrival in the colony, situated on a small peninsula called Port Arthur, and separated from the mainland by a very narrow isthmus.

Across this, called Eagle Hawk Neck, there was placed a line of savage dogs, each one chained to a kennel with just sufficient length of chain to prevent anyone passing through the cordon without being seized, and at the same time short enough to prevent the dogs fighting each other.*

What strides have been made since then! Whether greater by sea or land appears doubtful; but one thing is certain—that the last forty years has produced more change on both elements than the previous hundred. In the year 1772 Captain Cook started on his voyage of discovery in a vessel of four hundred and sixty tons—about the same size as those that were in use at the time I have treated of; and I need not remind the reader of the immense growth in the size of ships since then. The time consumed in going from one part of the world to another has also been altered in a no less remarkable manner.

If to those who, at the present day, would shrink from trusting their lives and comforts for a long voyage to any vessel of less than three or four thousand tons, a ship of only five hundred tons, such as I have already mentioned, seems uncomfortable, if not hazardous, what will they say when I mention that the vessel on board of which I returned to England

* Two works giving a vivid picture of convict life in Australia have appeared—*The Broad Arrow*, and *For the Term of his Natural Life*, by the late Marcus Clarke

measured only two hundred and eight tons—probably about the same size as the largest boat carried on board some of the leviathan steamers of the present day.

But, however hazardous they may think it, I believe that so far from any extra danger being incurred from sailing in these small ships, it was not only as safe, but, judging from the accounts we read of the damage sustained by these monsters of the deep in heavy weather, the balance may be in favour of the smaller craft. They were so buoyant that they rose with the waves instead of going through them, and, like the little "Eudora," in which I made the homeward voyage, were like a duck upon the water.

In my own case, the small size of the ship had a special advantage, as I was allowed to take the wheel whenever I liked, which could hardly have been the case in a large one ; and really the steering her over the grand waves in the Pacific and Atlantic Oceans in half a gale of wind was not very much inferior to driving a racing coach.

One day, however, I was let in for rather more than I bargained for. It was blowing an increasingly heavy gale off Cape Horn, such as it knows how to blow in that part of the world in winter, and the hands were all aloft taking in sail, when the skipper turned to me and said, " I wish you would take the wheel and send the man forward, as I want more strength aloft." Thus the whole crew were in the rigging, and if by any mistake I had allowed the sail they were reefing to fill, they must have been carried overboard with it.

It may seem rather a happy-go-lucky way of sending a ship to sea, for the crew to be so short-handed as to make it necessary to call in the aid of a passenger in such an emergency, but those were the "pre-Plimsoll days," and before ships' masters and other officers were subjected to examinations. In one ship on board which I sailed, the owner was overheard to say to a friend who had accompanied him on board, " With such a captain and such a mate, I only wonder the ship ever comes home safe again."

If we return to the other element we shall see that though improvements had taken place, to some extent, as early as the beginning of this century, still little had been effected before the year 1820. From that date great improvements were made in every-thing connected with road travelling, so much so, that we in England congratulated ourselves that it had pretty well arrived at perfection, when, lo and behold! a new power asserted itself, and produced such a metamorphosis that few persons not exceeding fifty years of age have ever taken a long road journey in their lives. Road travelling is as much a thing of the past as "pigtails," and if it were not for the few coaches running in the summer from Hatchett's and other places in London, the shape of such a thing would be forgotten by most people. As it is, those give but a slight notion of what a long coach used to look like when commencing its journey of 150 or 200 miles.

It would be looked upon as a curiosity if one was placed in the Baker Street Bazaar, or some other suitable site, loaded as they used to be. Probably there are not twenty of us now living who have put one of these loads on with our own hands, or would have any idea of how to build it up.

THE EXTRA COACH AT CHRISTMAS.

The loads, especially about Christmas, on the night coaches used to be "prodigious," as Dominie Samson would have said. An inexperienced eye would almost expect the coach to collapse under them when the load was of such dimensions that the ordinary luggage strap was not long enough to span the pile, but had to be supplemented with what was called a lengthening strap, which consisted of a strap about four feet long, with a buckle at one end, and the whole length perforated with holes.

Nothing saved them but their admirable construction, which combined the greatest strength with moderate weight ; those built to carry the heaviest loads seldom exceeding a ton or twenty-two hundredweight, and the perch being short was favourable to draught. For a great many years they were nearly all perch coaches, as it was pretty well the universal opinion that under-spring coaches were not so steady or well calculated for heavy loads and high speed.

This opinion, however, was in later years considerably modified, and most coachmen that I was acquainted with had arrived at a conclusion favourable to the under-spring build. I can say this for them, that the fastest work I ever did was on one of them, and also that the heaviest load I ever drove was on another of that description ; and I cannot but " speak well of the bridges which carried me safe over," for they performed their journeys admirably. They certainly possess the advantage of weighing two or three hundredweight less, and, from the splinter-bar being higher, the line of draught from the wheel horses' collars to the roller bolts is straighter. Though they are lighter, they lose nothing in strength when originally so constructed ; but I would not recommend anyone to convert a perch coach, as I once did so with the result that the front boot came away from the body.

the present day which would not have found favour
fifty years ago, and, though I will not venture to say
that no changes have taken place for the better since
then, I would call to mind the fact, that as driving was
then the real business of life to thousands, and that
coachmen at that time had a much more extensive
practice than can be obtained now, the presumption is
that they were likely to have found out the right way
to go to work. Indeed, there were *artists* in those
days—men who would drive any brute that could be
harnessed, and could get any load through the country
at almost any pace and in all weathers, by night or
day.

But before going further on this subject, perhaps
it will be better to lay a foundation.

Before horses can be driven satisfactorily they must
be properly put together, and to this end everyone
who aspires to be a coachman should have a practical
knowledge of how his team should be harnessed and
"put to the coach." It has been truly remarked that
horses well put together are half driven.

Now, first, for a few faults, one of the greatest of
which, and one not very uncommon, is to have the
pole chains too slack. If they are hooked so that
there is no strain upon them when the traces are tight,
they are slack enough, and more than that is bad,
as it takes away the power of the horses over the
coach and of the coachman over the horses, and has

oftener than generally supposed been the cause of a kicking bout, as I have endeavoured to show in a previous chapter.

The London " 'bus men" do have their pole chains very slack, and they are right, because their horses are continually falling upon the slippery streets, and it gives them room to struggle and get up again with little danger of breaking the pole ; but this does not apply to road work, and there, if the pace is very fast, it is dangerous from its tendency to make the coach rock.

I am always puzzled when I see coachmen driving with the present fashion of long coupling reins. What good can they see in them ? Here again the 'bus men, who I suppose set the example, have reason on their side. They sometimes require to alter a coupling rein on the journey, and, from being able to reach the buckle from their seat, can do so at any stopping, without help from the conductor, who is engaged with the passengers ; but this can never be necessary with a gentleman's drag or a coach. In the one case there is the groom, and in the other, the guard, to do what is required—that is to say, in the latter case, if there is time to do anything at all, for I recollect on one occasion having to drive an eleven mile stage in an hour, when the horsekeeper had carelessly reversed the reins by putting the leading draught one's inside and the coupling reins outside, but the pace was too good to alter. It appears to me that the long coupling reins only add to the weight, which is necessarily considerable, without conferring any benefit, and, indeed, when, as I have seen them, they are so long that the buckle touches the left hand, they can hardly be unattended with danger.

When I first learned driving scarcely anyone thought of going without bearing reins, they were considered by all, except a few who were looked upon as innovators, to be as necessary as the traces. Their utility, however, soon began to be questioned, and they rapidly came into disuse in the coaches, and no doubt horses do work easier to themselves without them, especially with heavy loads and fast pace. Still they are of use occasionally, and I have employed a slack one to the cheek of the bit when a horse has a trick of throwing out his head and snatching at his reins, and so making it impossible to prevent his rein slipping through the fingers, which should never occur.

I believe that bearing reins may also be useful, and indeed a security (though as a general rule I hate them) when, as is the fashion now, a pair of high-bred powerful horses are put to draw a Victoria or some other very light carriage, for doubtless a bit does act more powerfully when accompanied by a bearing rein than without one.

I dare say I shall be thought very old fashioned,

but I do not think that horses do generally go as
pleasantly to the coachman with such very light
weights behind them, as when there is weight enough
to make them feel their collars. A team, to go
pleasantly, should have a load proportioned to its
power, so that they may have something to pull at
besides the coachman's hand. It must be admitted
also in their favour, that bearing reins do prevent
wheel horses rubbing and scratching their bridles
against the pole chains when standing still.

Like many other old established institutions, they
continued to have their advocates for a long time, and
by some very competent judges bearing reins were
considered necessary for safety, as will appear from the
anecdote I am about to narrate. When they were
first being dispensed with, Ned Cracknell, who drove
a Birmingham day coach called the " Triumph," left
them off. Upon the coach arriving at Hounslow one
day, who should be standing there but Mr. Chaplin,
commonly known as Billy Chaplin, the proprietor out
of London, and before Cracknell had time to get on
his box, though they were very quick in changing at
Hounslow, he observed that there were no bearing
reins, and only snaffle bits in the horses' mouths,
whereupon he called out, " Hallo, Mr. Cracknell, what
monkey tricks are these you are playing ? If you don't
put on the curb bits and the bearing reins, you don't
take the 'Triumph' coach out of the 'Swan with

Two Necks' again." Probably he was quite right
about the snaffle bits, as the following instance will
show :—

Seven mail coaches used to leave the "White
Horse Cellars" every evening, and at one time there
was a great rivalry between the Devonport mail,
commonly called the "Quicksilver," driven by Captain
Davies, and the Stroud mail, driven by Harry Downs,
a broken-down gentleman, for here I may remark,
though it is a fact well known to most people, that in
those days it was no uncommon thing to see well-bred
men driving stage-coaches. But to return. As the
Stroud mail with four bright bays, and the "Quicksilver" with four bright chestnuts, were racing at a
very merry pace, our friend Harry's bays, having only
snaffle bits, bolted across Turnham Green, which
would probably be a feat incapable of accomplishment
now, and an old friend of mine, who was travelling by
it, and by the bye a very good coachman himself, says,
" I experienced a very unsmooth journey until we
reached the road again, and by that time the 'Quicksilver' was through Brentford."

Of late years there has sprung up a fancy that
blinkers are not only unnecessary, but absolutely an
evil, and a good deal of newspaper correspondence
has been the result, without going very far towards
elucidating the subject. So far as I am able to
understand the controversy, the opponents of blinkers

consider they have proved their case when they tell us that horses, when accustomed to it, are not frightened by seeing the carriage behind them, and that therefore there can be no danger in going without them. That horses can be used to seeing the carriage behind them without taking fright, there can be no doubt, but that by no means ends the question. Those on the other side say, and with truth, that in double harness, when the bridles are without blinkers, one horse does occasionally, either from tossing his head or some other cause, injure the eye of the other one by striking it with the cheek of the bit. A well-fitting blinker is no discomfort to a horse, and I think I can bring forward a case which will go very far to prove that they may be of great use.

One evening when I was driving the " Harkaway " coach on the down journey, when within about a mile from Dolgelly, as we rounded a sharpish corner of the road, the leaders caught sight of some boards which had been left, very improperly, on the near side of the road, and were so much frightened at the sight that they bolted right across to the other side of the road, and, that being rather narrow, it was as much as I could do to prevent the coach running into the off-side hedge, which would most certainly have ended in a spill, and probably have been attended with very disastrous consequences, for, as was usual in summer, there was a good load of passengers and luggage.

16

We must recollect that a horse, from the position of his eye, has the power of seeing a long way behind him, which is necessary to his safety in a wild state, as he depends very largely for defence upon his heels ; consequently, any object which alarms him continues in sight for a long time, and in the case I have just mentioned, i am certain that if they could have seen the object of their terror another moment, nothing I could have done would have saved an accident.

Perhaps I shall be told that if these horses had never been driven in blinkers they would not have shied at the boards ; to which I can only answer that saddle horses which have never had their sight restricted in their lives are by no means free from the fault of shying.   As I have already remarked, a well-fitting blinker can cause no discomfort to a horse, as it presses upon and rubs no part of the head, and, to say the least of it, they may be a great safeguard against accidents.

With regard to those other parts of the harness now more or less disused, what shall be said ?   Well, a good deal will depend upon circumstances.   Where there is no bearing rein a crupper may not be necessary upon level roads if the pads are well shaped ; but if they are not, or the road is hilly, those on the wheel horses may work forward and wound the withers.   With leaders this is less likely to occur, for their reins run in a straight line through the pad territs; but the reins, taking a turn from the wheel pad territs up to the coachman's hand, have a tendency to work those pads forward.

I have used a light pad for leaders made without a tree, which is what I like best for them, and which, from fitting closer to the horses' backs, hardly can work forward, and they are less likely to rub the withers if they do; but probably this make would not be strong enough for wheel harness except upon level ground, where there is very little holding back. I must confess that I do hold to the old lines,

> " Here's to the arm which can hold 'em when gone,
>   Still to a gallop inclined, sir ;
>   Heads in the front without bearing reins on,
>   And tails with no cruppers behind, sir."

Without wheel pads the coachman must lose power immensely. He has not only lost the leverage caused by the change of direction of the reins from the pads to his hand, but he can hardly have his horses so well in hand but that he will require to shorten his reins through his left hand if, from any cause, he wants to get a stronger pull upon his horses; and this, in my humble opinion, is inadmissible in really good driving, except upon very rare exceptions.

I fear I shall meet with a good deal of dissent to this statement, and can fancy that already I hear some one saying that it is impossible. Doubtless it is not easy, and requires much practice, more, perhaps, than can fall to the lot of most men now-a-days ; but that it is possible I know, as I think I can make out clearly at a future time.

Half a century ago I do not remember ever to have seen leading reins run anywhere except over the heads of the wheel horses, between the ears.

Perhaps it was rather rough on the wheel horses to keep their heads up with the bearing rein, and then put the weight of a pulling leader's rein on the top of it ; but there is a good deal to be said in favour of head territs, and when horses are allowed to carry their heads as low as they like, the principal objection to them is removed ; and they certainly help to keep the leading reins higher, and therefore less likely to be caught under a leader's tail, which sets some horses kicking, and, at any rate, interferes with the running of the rein.   When leading reins are run through the throat latch, they are very easily caught by the tail, and when this is done, the best thing I have found to keep the rein clear of a kicking leader is to pass both leading reins through a ring, and then run the kicker's rein through the inside of the wheeler's throat latch. I have seen the leader's rein run through the outside of his bar, but fancy the other method is better.

Occasionally a wheel horse will make himself exceedingly objectionable to the one in front of him be tossing his head, and I once had a case of this sort

J. Sturgess del. et lith.

ONCE MORE RUNNING A STEEPLE CHASE.

M&N. Hanhart. imp.

so bad that the leader's mouth had no peace. I ran
the rein direct from his pad to the wheel hame territ,
and concord was at once established.

Before leaving the subject of the ribbons, perhaps
I may as well touch upon the subject of "pinning
them." Shall they be pinned or shall they not be
pinned ? It is not a subject of so much interest now
as it used to be, since, whether on a private drag or a
modern coach, there is generally time enough to
buckle and unbuckle ; but in former days this was
not always the case, for in very fast work there was
not a moment to spare. Is then the practice of going
without the buckle dangerous or not ? Nimrod, in his
article in the *Quarterly Review* denounced it, calling
it a "mere piece of affectation." A Postmaster-
General also denounced the practice as being the
cause of accidents. Of course, if the reins are short,
which they ought not to be, there is the danger of
their being drawn through the hand, but the plan I
have adopted in such a case has been to tie a knot in
the end of the rein, so that it was impossible for it to
slip out of my hand.

And now, having quoted two high authorities in
favour of pinning, I will cite the same number of
instances which tend to favour the other side of the
question. The first occurred to the Gloucester and
Aberystwith mail about forty years ago when on its
down journey, and was a rather curious incident.

When the mail changed horses at Torrington, just as it was starting, the leaders, both old steeplechasers, named Blue Bonnet and Cleanthus, sprang off with such force as to break the pole-hook, and, of course, took the swinging bars with them, and the leading reins went through the coachman's hand with the rapidity of lightning. Fortunately, however, these were not buckled, and the horses got off clear, perhaps indulging in the idea that they were once more running a steeplechase, and so they continued their career till they arrived at the toll-gate at Stoke Edith, which, trying to jump, they broke into atoms, at the same time clearing themselves of most of the harness, indeed, all except the bridles and collars, and were found some time afterwards grazing quietly by the side of the road. Now if the reins had been buckled it would have been impossible for the coachman to unbuckle them quick enough to allow the horses to get clear off, and an accident of a very serious nature would most likely have happened, as, it being an election day, the mail was very heavily loaded with passengers and luggage.

The other case occurred to a coach which we put on in summer between Dolgelly and Machynlleth as a sort of auxiliary to the "Harkaway." It was only a three-horse power, and one morning on the up journey the leader was so alarmed by a dog running and barking at him that he sprang round suddenly, and the

J. Sturgess del. et lith.

M&N. Hanhart imp.

MET THE LOOSE HORSE TEARING DOWN THE HILL.

bar very fortunately twisted out of the pole-hook as he did so; and Jack Andrews, who was driving, not having buckled his reins, had only got to let them run through his fingers to release him entirely from the coach. As I was following with the "Harkaway" about half a mile behind, I was astonished to meet the loose horse tearing down the hill towards us, terrified by the bar banging about his houghs and the reins dangling at his heels, I feared I should shortly come upon a smash, which certainly must have been the case if the horse had not been able to go away clear of the coach. And now, gentle readers, I leave you to take your choice, premising that, for myself, I lean to unpinned ribbons.

Perhaps it may not be generally known now that, long years ago, in the days of the slow and heavy, it was the custom to use what was called "the short wheel rein;" that is, they were just long enough to hook upon the finger. In those days, also, coachmen did not catch their whips, only giving the thong a few turns round the crop at the upper ferrule.

Having now, I think, said enough on the subject of harness, we are ready to proceed to mounting the box.

Nimrod has somewhere said that a good coachman could almost be perceived by the manner in which he put his gloves on, or words to that effect; but without going so far as that, I believe the way in which he mounts his box is no bad criterion. How different to see a practised hand approach his team with confidence, and the almost mechanical way in which he handles the reins, from the hesitation and fumbling so often apparent in a tyro. Let us picture him to ourselves as he approaches his horses, how easily he catches his whip, the crop held well up so as not to run the chance of the thong being entangled in the wheeler's ears, and there are no festoons of the thong. Then taking hold with the left hand of the leading reins, nearly up at the territs, beginning with the near side, he gives them a pull sufficient to satisfy himself that no impediment exists to their free running, and passes them to the centre finger of the right hand ; after which, doing the same with the wheel reins, he places them on the forefinger of the right hand, in which position they are ready to be transferred to the left hand, only reversing the fingers. This will prevent any necessity for sorting the reins after having mounted the box, and thus enabling him to start without a moment's delay. The other two fingers should be tightly pressed upon the reins to prevent them slipping.

I should not have entered into all this minutiæ if I had not seen, on one or two occasions, the reins divided by placing one finger between the two near-side reins, and the other between the off-side ones. Then there is another form to be equally deprecated,

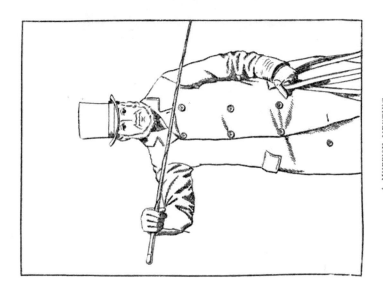

A MUFFISH MEETING.

A NEAT MEETING.

To face p. 248.

which, though seldom seen in double reins, is far too
common with those driving a pair, or in single harness.
I mean the thumb pressed down upon the reins and
pointing to the front, a position which must inevitably
pin the elbow to the side, and be destructive of all
strength.

But I have seen what is even worse. I once
beheld a gentleman performing in Hyde Park, who,
finding himself seriously incommoded with the slack
of his reins, stretched out his right hand over the left,
seizing the reins in front of it, and then, like sailors
hauling a rope hand over hand, proceeding to pass
his left hand to the front and take hold of them
in front of the right hand. I have frequently
seen this manœuvre practised by coachmen driving
one, or a pair, but only this once did I see the
trick played on a four-horse box, and I should
think, when it was completed, that the reins must
have very much resembled a pack of cards well
shuffled, and admirably calculated to land the coach in
a ditch after dark.

If there is leisure for looking carefully over each
horse before starting, the strain upon the reins, as
previously recommended, is not necessary, but when
every moment of time is of importance, that is quite
impossible, and especially is it so at night, but for all
practical purposes it will generally be found sufficient;
and to try and point my moral, I will mention what

happened to one of the best coachmen I ever saw handle the ribbons.

One evening, after dark, Charles Tustin, with the up Aberystwith and Shrewsbury mail, as he was driving out of Newtown, found when he wanted to turn at the end of the first street, that the near wheel draught rein would not run, and consequently the coach came in collision with the corner shop.

Now if he had taken a pull at his reins, as I have ventured to recommend, and as I have little doubt he usually did, he would have found out that the horsekeeper had carelessly fastened the rein in question between the hame and the collar. He was too good a coachman not to make the least of an accident, and no harm happened to anything except the glass in the shop window.

There is, however, one exception to this rule, which is that some horses are so exceedingly nervous that if they find out when the coachman is mounting his box, they are immediately all over the road, and these must be humoured.

It is very important that the reins should be so arranged in the right hand before leaving the ground that they can be transferred to the left in working order immediately upon placing both feet on the footboard, for some horses will brook no delay ; and if

the coachman is not at once in a position to say, " Let
'em go, and take care of yourselves," almost before
he is seated, there may be a jibbing bout, or a mess of
some sort. With some teams it is, or at any rate
used to be

> " If you will not when you may,
> When you will you shall have nay."

I had at one time a leader of so nervous a tem-
perament, though very good tempered, that, having to
pull up to take up a passenger in the street just after
leaving the inn yard, and where a brass band was
playing, he reared so high, that in his descent he fell
clean over his partner, but, as he had no vice, no
injury was sustained except some slight breakages to
the harness.

On being " put to " on one occasion he so alarmed
the box passenger that he took only one step from the
footboard to " terra firma," and if he had not been
nearly as quick in getting back he must have been
left behind, as it was my taking up the reins and
mounting the box which started the horse off in his
capers.

With such horses as these, when the rein is run
and the inside trace hooked, it is time to be off, and
the horsekeeper must hook the other as best he can,
but if the coachman is not smart with his reins he
cannot do it.

I hope I shall not weary the reader with these

digressions, and make him exclaim, "What an egotistical old ass he is," but as I do not pretend to say that no improvements have taken place in the art of driving during the last forty or fifty years, I am endeavouring to enforce my recommendations with facts which have occurred to myself or those I have known.

CHAPTER XXIII.

DRIVING.

WELL, the ideal coachman is now on his box, and I hope with straight knees, feet close together, and well out in front of him, shoulders well thrown back, and arms hanging naturally, and without any effort, to his sides. The left arm should be straight or nearly so, and hand lightly resting against the outside of the left thigh, with the wrist slightly rounded and the thumb a little turned up ; that is to say, when the horses are drawing. The difference between his hand when in this position and when the elbow is bent and the hand brought up towards the body, should be just the difference between slack and tight pole-chains. When more power is wanted the hand will be raised and the wrist turned so as to bring the back of the hand to the front. This will throw the elbow a little forward, which will add greatly to the strength of the arm, and by this time the right hand would most probably have taken hold of the off-side reins, which of itself lends much to the power of the other.

I fear I may have made myself but imperfectly

understood, but perhaps the accompanying sketches may assist in explaining what I mean.

The reins, by right, should never be allowed to slip through the fingers. It looks bad, to say the least of it, to see a coachman shortening them, and, at night especially, is not safe.

I know that this is not easy to do, and perhaps impossible to most amateurs, as it requires constant practice to give the necessary strength to the fingers, and the difficulty is much enhanced by well cleaned reins, especially if they are thin.

I know that many good coachmen differ with me as to the position of the left arm, and, like a dear old friend of mine, and good coachman, now no more, say that a straight arm is not neat. For myself I am unable to see the want of neatness in it; but even if there is I cannot consent to sacrifice strength, and I am convinced that no man can, under all circumstances, be thoroughly powerful on his box, who drives habitually with a bent arm.

With the fear of being called egotistical before my eyes, I will again endeavour to enforce what I have advanced by a case in point.

One afternoon on the down journey with the "Harkaway," when within about a mile from Dolgelly, the skid-pan, though nearly a new one, broke off at the neck, and the force of the jerk upon the safety hook broke that also. The whole weight

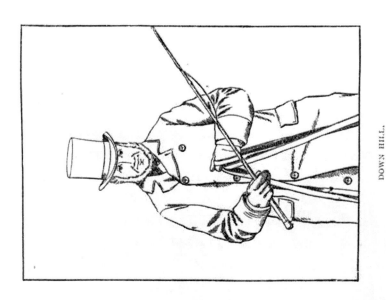

A SUDDEN EMERGENCY.

DOWN HILL.

To face p. 254.

of the load consequently, and it was a bumper, came immediately upon the necks of the wheel horses, naturally somewhat startling them ; and if I had lost hold of their heads for a second, they would most likely have been frightened, and refused to hold, when there would have been nothing but galloping for it, but by having the left arm in the position I have endeavoured to explain, I was enabled at the same moment to apply the brake, and keep a firm hold of the horses' heads.

It is from driving with a bent arm that one hears people say they cannot work their own brakes. If I had been in that form on the occasion I have mentioned, I must first of all have used the right hand to shorten the reins through the left, before I could have employed it to put on the brake. As it was, the wheelers landed the coach down the hill without serious difficulty, though one of them was only four years old, and by no means a strong holder.

I cannot understand how any coachman can like to have his brake worked for him. The want of it differs so much from day to day, depending upon the load, the state of the road and other causes, that nothing but his own left hand can tell him how to work it. I am sure I should have been impossible to please. It is a most invaluable thing when properly used, but is very liable to be abused. Few things are more aggravating than to see it so applied as to cause horses to draw down hill, as I have often witnessed. The change from drawing to holding back, brings fresh muscles into play, and must therefore be a great relief to horses, as we know the change from up hill to down, and vice versa, is to us when walking.

Before leaving the subject of reins, which may be called the "key of the position," I would venture to raise my voice against what is too often done, which is to pass the right hand across to pull the near side reins. Hands across is very proper in a country dance, but a little of it goes a long way in driving. It is more honoured in the breach than in the observance.

If the team is well "put together" and the reins are properly held in the left hand, the wrist should be sufficiently supple to lift a near wheel horse nearly off his legs.

It is a good test that all is as it should be if, upon pulling up to unskid, the wheelers will back the coach off the skid-pan without any difficulty. Of course, the right hand must be used to the off-side reins, which itself is a help to the left, but no shortening of the reins through the fingers of the left hand should be wanted, and to reach the right hand out to grasp the reins in front of the left, as I have seen done, is absolutely insufferable.

I was once talking on this subject to Charles Tustin, with whose name I have already taken liberties, when he remarked that a coachman should

THE TEAM GATHERED.

THE TEAM EXTENDED.

To face p. 256.

take up his reins at the beginning of a stage, and
never have to alter them in his left hand till he throws
them down at the end of it. Some drivers I have
seen appear to think it a sign of a light hand to be
constantly fiddling with the reins. I believe it is more
a sign of a fidgeting hand, and I am quite sure, from
experience, that hot-tempered horses settle down much
better without it. The less their mouths are meddled
with the better.

There is one use, however, to which the right hand
may sometimes be applied, which is to take hold
of the near lead rein and loop it up under the left
thumb upon turning a sharp corner to the left, and
also if a near wheel horse throws himself against the
pole in going down hill or pulling up, to do the same
with his rein. From the position a horse in this
posture has placed his pad territs in, the rein will
naturally become slack and useless, and by shortening
it in the way I have described, the left arm resumes
its power, and, what is of nearly as much importance,
the right is free to use the whip, which will probably
be wanted at such a crisis.

One hint may not be out of place here as it
may not have occurred to some, and that is, when
bringing up the right hand to take hold of the off-
side reins, not to reach forward with it, but to bring
it up just touching the left, and to seize the reins
immediately below that hand. The right hand can

17

then be passed along the reins as far as is necessary, placing a finger to separate the lead and wheel, when either can be pulled separately as may be required.

This may seem to some so small a thing, as not to be worth bothering about, but it is by attending to minutiæ that the accomplished coachman is made ; neither is it of such very small importance, as I have known a coach upset for want of its being attended to, and it is especially necessary at night when everything is done by feel.

Old Griffie Williams, as honest a fellow as ever lived, but not the most accomplished of coachmen, who for many summers partly horsed and drove the " Tourist " coach between Aberystwith and Dolgelly, when descending a hill on his up journey, wanted to pull his horses out of the near side of the road, and, reaching forward too far with his right hand, he took up the near wheel rein together with the off-side ones. Of course, the more he pulled at the reins the harder he pulled the near wheeler towards the near side of the road, and it ended in the wheels running up the hedge bank, and putting the coach on its side into the road.

Fortunately he was, as usual, going slowly, and very little harm was done to anyone. Upon my asking him afterwards how he came to scatter his passengers, he replied, " Inteed, I was put them down as nice as was go to bed."

Young coachmen may possibly mistake the weight

inseparable from four-horse reins from having got them too tight, but upon looking they may see that the curb-chains are slack, and if that is the case the reins are not too tight. It is not desirable to hold horses too hard, but if a lot of slack is out a coachman is helpless if a horse falls or anything else goes wrong. Moreover, horses generally go better for being well held together. A coachman driving a coach, such as they used to be, who loosed his horses' heads, was generally soon brought to the use of his whip, whilst the same horses, well held together, would be fresh at the end of their stage.

I can now call to mind an instance of this. About half a century ago it was a common lounge in Shrewsbury for those whose time was not fully occupied, to collect at the top of the Wyle Cop, where the "Lion Hotel" was situated, to see the "Hirondelle" and "Hibernia," Liverpool and Cheltenham coaches, come up the hill, and perhaps sometimes a bet might be made as to which would be first, for they did a good deal of racing. Of course, I never let the opportunity slip when I was in that ancient borough of forming one of this number.

The late Mr. Isaac Taylor had, at that time, a team of chestnuts as good as could be put to a coach working in the "Hirondelle" on the down side between Shrewsbury and Leighton, a stage of about eight miles. Little Bob Leek, a very clever coachman, used to drive the up side from Shrewsbury, and Jordan, a very powerful man, the down side. When they met they changed coaches, each returning over his own ground, which he drove double. Shrewsbury was, I believe, the correct place for the coaches to meet at, but, as the opposition was keen, it depended on the racing whether they met in Shrewsbury or a few miles on either side of it; and I have seen this same team driven by Jordan, and when he was hard at work with his whip to get up the hill, ascend it another day when driven by Bob Leek with ease, and he sitting on his box as if he had nothing to do. And, strange as it may appear to some, I believe one of the best tests that can be applied to a coachman is that he should appear to do nothing. I suppose, however, that this rule applies to most other crafts, for what a man does well he does easily to himself, and one who is always hard at work may be set down as a muff. I know from experience that this rule applies to steering a ship. If a helmsman is seen to be constantly at work with the wheel, it is a sure proof that he is not a good hand at it. Just the movement of a spoke or two occasionally is generally enough in the hands of a good helmsman.

And now I will bring the subject of driving to an end by giving a few hints, which, though simple in themselves, and probably known to many of my readers, may not have suggested themselves to some modern coachmen, for the simple reason that they have never felt the want of them, but which were well known to those coachmen whose business it was to get a coach through a country with all sorts of cattle, and when every little dodge was a help.

One of the commonest evils which befell coachmen was to deal with jibbers, they caused the loss of so much time. A kicker, especially if a well-bred one, would kick and keep going too, but a jibber sometimes stuck to the same ground if not got off with the first attempt. As a rule, flogging is of no use, though I have a few times in my life succeeded in making it too hot for them ; and, of course, with three good starters one wheeler may be dragged on if he does not lie down. Sometimes, however, a whole team was not to be trusted.

I was once travelling from Aberystwith to Oswestry by the " Engineer " coach, and, as usual, was working, when, upon nearing Machynlleth, Wigram, the coachman, said to me, " You will find the next a good team, but they are all jibbers." I asked him if any one of them was a better starter than the others, to which he replied, " Well, perhaps the off wheeler is a little." The hint was sufficient, and as soon as I was on the box I laid the whip quietly over the off wheeler before trying to start the others, and then immediately pulling the leaders across

to the near side, and at the same time speaking to
them, the start was effected without any trouble.

Perhaps it may be thought by some that this was
no very great test, as the horses were always what
was called " running home," that is, they had always
their own stable at each end of the stage. At the
risk, therefore, of tiring the reader and being accused
of egotism, I will venture to mention one other case
where there was no assistance from that cause ; and as
a failure to start makes a fellow look foolish, there can
be no harm in impressing upon the minds of young
coachmen what will, in nine cases out of ten, save
them from being placed in such a situation.

I was quartered with my regiment, the 72nd
Highlanders, in the Royal Barracks, Dublin, so many
years ago that the Garrison Steeplechases were run off
at Maynooth instead of Punchestown as at present,
and we had got up a regimental drag for the occasion,
of which I was waggoner. As we were starting to
return home, the off wheeler jibbed, much to the
delight of the Paddies, who had come there for a day's
" divarshun," and had some fun in them in those days.
Of course, a small crowd was fast collected, and
everyone was giving advice and wanting to help,
the old Irishman's remedy of lighting a fire under him
not being forgotten. I made everyone stand clear,
and would not allow anybody to touch a horse, and
then, after giving them a minute or two to settle down,

I laid the whip lightly over the near wheeler, and then pulling the leaders across to the off side, spoke to them, and we were off in a jiffy. The pulling the leaders across is very important, as it greatly facilitates the draught.

There is also another good result which frequently follows the pulling of the leaders across in case of a jibbing wheeler, which is, that as he will probably have only placed his legs with the view of resisting forward motion, a sudden rough lateral bump of the pole may disconcert his plans and render it necessary for him to move his feet, in which case he is more than half conquered, unless, indeed, he lies down, which the coachman should be too quick to permit.

I think I have already remarked that flogging makes flogging, especially if the horses' heads are loosed too much. It adds, no doubt, somewhat to the labour of the coachman, but for all that he should always keep a good hold of his horses' heads, and a pull of the reins and then giving back again I have often found more efficacious than a good deal of whip. This movement used sometimes to be called by the uncomplimentary name of the " Blackguard's Snatch," but, in spite of an ugly name, it often had salutary results, and with a weak team, heavy load, and time to keep, a coachman could not afford to despise anything.

I have known sluggish leaders very much

astonished when hit on the inside.   Having only been accustomed to the punishment coming from the outside, they do not know what to make of it when coming from another quarter.   It is not difficult to hit the near leader from behind the off pretty sharply, but it is by no means easy to do the same on the other side.   It requires the elbow to be well raised, and the back of the hand turned well downwards, for, of course, the thong must be sent under the bars.   If done well these are very neat hits.

Very hard-pulling leaders are often easier brought back by sending the other one well up to them than by pulling at them.   I have had a raking leader, irritated by a very slow partner, try to bolt, and by hitting his partner have brought him back directly ; but he must be "hit sly," so as to make no noise with the whip.   The same thing will occur when a hard-pulling leader has a harder puller put alongside him— he comes back at once.

With two leaders of unequal strength it is a good plan to cross the inside traces.   It is an assistance to the weaker one, and tends to keep the coach straight.

Check reins are often of use to bring these sort of horses together, and I have, with a very hard puller, had a long one from his nose-band back to the pole-hook.

Lastly, what about kickers, which were, perhaps, the most numerous of all the reprobates that found

their way into coaches. I have known a short stick
placed between the bottom of the collar and the
horse's jaws so as to keep the head raised, in which
position he cannot kick badly ; but I never used one
myself, as I never knew a good dose or two of counter
irritation over the ears fail to make a sufficient cure of
a wheel horse to enable him to be driven, and a little
kicking by a leader does not so much signify if he will
keep moving at the same time.

There was an old saying, " Point your leaders and
shoot your wheelers," which, perhaps, some of the
younger generation may not have heard. It does
not very often require to be put in practice, especially
at the present time, as it is only really necessary in
awkward turns, such as the " Swan with Two Necks,"
in Lad Lane, in former days, and, more recently, the
" Belle Vue " yard at Aberystwith. Of course, there
were many more, but these two will suffice as
specimens of what I mean. The latter I have known
a coachman of long experience fail to get into, in
consequence, as I suppose, of his not observing this
precept.

To get into this yard two turns had to be taken in
a very limited space. The first was to the left, into a
street just about wide enough for two coaches to pass,
and as soon as the coach and horses were straight
after completing this turn, it was time to point the
leaders to the right for the narrow entrance to the

yard, and if that operation was not accompanied by a shoot of the wheelers to the left, the off hind wheel would not pass clear of the gate post.

This "shoot" is a momentary thing, and should be done by a twist of the left wrist. If the right hand is called in to assist it looks bad. More like a man playing the harp than driving four horses, and, moreover, it is wanted to the off-side reins at the same time.

If the turns are in the contrary direction, of course the manipulation of the reins must be done with the right hand.

The "point and shoot" would be a great assistance at an "obstacle contest."

While on the subject of turns, perhaps I may be allowed to offer another small hint, which, though stale news to many, may be a useful wrinkle for others. It is a good plan, when rounding a sharp corner with a top-heavy load, to make the turn so as to place the outside wheels as much as possible on the crest of the road. This can be effected, if the angle is to the left, by keeping near to the off-side of the road as you approach the bend, and then making a rather short turn so as to hug the near side hedge, by which means the outside wheels will be placed on the highest part of the road, just when the coach most requires the support, and this also gives the coachman more freedom in case of his meeting any vehicle in the middle

of the turn. Should the angle be to the right instead
of the left, the principle is just the same.

There yet remain two or three other subjects connected with driving, which, though of comparatively
little importance in the present day, must, nevertheless,
be taken into account in the making of a perfect
" waggoner :" these are the power of using the whip
and a capacity to judge of pace.

We commonly hear a man called a good whip,
thereby meaning a good coachman; but the fact is that
comparatively few coachmen in the present day use
their whips really well, for the simple reason that they
are not called upon to do so.   Still the necessity might
arise, and then the power of doing so might save
an accident. At any rate, a man who can only use one
arm is but half a coachman.

From what I have said on previous occasions, it
will not, I think, be supposed that I am an advocate
for " hitting 'em all round," but in days of yore no man
could be considered really safe who was not able to
hit when necessary, and to hit hard.

I received an early lesson on this subject when I
was at work on the Birmingham and Manchester
Express, taking a lesson from Wood, who was my first
mentor.   There was at off wheel what was called a
" stiff-necked one " that no pulling at was able to turn
if he took it into his head to resist, and I was helplessly
approaching a coal cart, when Wood said, " Why don't

you hit him?"   I obeyed the hint with so satisfactory
a result, that I have never since forgotten it, and have
to thank it for getting me out of accidents, one of
which at once recurs to my memory, and may perhaps
tend to impress it on the minds of others.

I was driving a coach on the Dover Road, and
as we were ascending Shooter's Hill a four-horse
posting job appeared coming towards us at a good
pace, when, upon pulling the reins to draw to the
near side of the road, I found that the off wheel horse
refused to obey them, and persistently hung to the
off side.   The posting job was coming nearer with
rapid strides.   The reins were evidently useless, and
it was a matter for the whip, whether I could hit hard
enough.   If I could not, nothing remained but to pull
up, and ignominiously beckon to the postboys to pass
on the wrong side.

However, I dropped into him with such effect that
he became in as great a hurry to cross the road as the
proverbial duck before thunder.   But perhaps this old
road joke may convey no meaning to many in the
present day, so I may as well explain.

It was a favourite conundrum, when some ducks
hurried across the road under the leaders' noses,
and apparently at the imminent risk of their lives,
" Why do ducks cross the road before thunder?"
Do you give it up?   Because they want to get to the
other side.

Perhaps I may be permitted here to introduce another old road story. A boy in charge of a sow and pigs was asked by a passenger the following question : " I say, my boy, whose pigs are those ? " *Boy.* "Why, that old sow's." *Querist.* "I don't mean that, you stupid boy. I want to know who's the master of them." *Boy.* " Oh, the maister of 'em ? why, that little sandy 'un. He's a deuce of a pig to fight."

But to return to ducks for just one minute. It is commonly said that it is impossible to run over a duck, and in truth, clumsy as they appear to be on their legs, it is very nearly so, though I did once accomplish the feat. I was driving fast round a rather sharp turn in the road, when I suddenly found myself in the middle of them, and one was unable to waddle off quick enough to save his life.

Then, again, to be a judge of pace, although of little importance now, should form part of a coachman's education. If a gentleman driving his private drag thinks he is going at the rate of twelve miles an hour when he is only going nine, it amuses him and hurts no one, neither is it very essential for those who drive the modern coaches from Hatchett's and other places. They, with few exceptions, only run by day, so that the coachman can consult his watch at every milestone if he likes, and the horsing is so admirable and the loading so light that he can experience no difficulty in picking up some lost time. In the old days, however, it was very different. If only five minutes were lost, it was often difficult to recover it with full loads and heavy roads, and, perhaps, weak teams. Moreover, at night the time-piece could only be seen at the different changes, and then, if the coachman was no judge of pace, he might easily find at the end of a ten miles' stage that he had lost five or ten minutes.

To be a good judge of pace requires experience, as the pace that horses appear to be going is very deceptive. When the draught is heavy horses step short, and, though their legs move as rapidly as usual, time is being lost, or at best only kept with difficulty ; whilst, on another day, when circumstances are different, load lighter and road hard, the horses step out, and the result is that over the same stage and with the same team, instead of losing time it is hardly possible to throw it away.

Again at night horses always seem to be going faster than they really are, and perhaps this may have had something to do with the idea that horses go better by night than day, so happily explained, as Mr. Reynoldson tells us, by Billy Williams, who said it was because the driver had had his dinner.

Apropos of Billy Williams, I may relate an anecdote of him, which I had from undeniable authority, but which I do not think is generally known.

His Honour, as he was called, the late Honourable Thomas Kenyon, used not unfrequently to ask him, or some other coachman, to spend a day or two at Pradoe, and he also made a practice of driving his own drag to Chester races on the Cup day. On one of these occasions it happened that Billy was at Pradoe, and was to accompany the party to Chester. The day being hot, and His Honour thinking that Billy, whose get up was always breeches and top boots, would be more comfortable in lighter clothing, made him a present of a pair of white trousers, such as were commonly worn by gentlemen of that period. Billy having received them, went to put them on, and returned looking quite smart and cool. It turned out, however, afterwards, that he had only worn them over his usual garments!

There remains one other item to mention, which, though not absolutely a part of driving, is yet of so much importance that without it all knowledge may fail at an important crisis.

Nerve is the article I mean, or what may be called the next door to it, that confidence which is begotten of practice. An inferior coachman with this is generally safer than one who is his superior in neatness and knowledge, but without this gift. When a man's nerve fails him, he loses his head, and then he is unable to make use of any knowledge he possesses, whereas, one with nerve and strength would pull through a difficulty and save an accident. Nerve, no doubt, is largely constitutional, but it is capable of being very much strengthened by use and practice.

But of all things to try nerve commend me to the locomotive engine.

Though I had driven coaches for many years under all imaginable circumstances, and my nerve had never failed me, I must confess that I never thoroughly understood what it meant till I had had the experience of a ride on a locomotive engine. To find myself travelling at a high speed, without there being the slightest power of guidance, caused a sensation I had never experienced before.

All that the engine-driver could have done, if a pointsman had made a mistake, was to try and stop the engine before it ran into anything else; whereas, on a road, when the driver has the power of guiding as well as stopping, if he is unable quite to accomplish the latter he may do so sufficiently to enable him to escape a collision.

To explain my meaning I will shortly narrate what has happened to myself.

I was driving rather fast over a nice level length of road, and was overtaking a waggon drawn by three or four horses. The waggoner very properly pulled to his own side of the road, and anticipating no difficulty I kept on at the pace I was previously going, but just as my leaders arrived within a short distance of the waggon, the horses overpowered the waggoner and crossed the road immediately in front of them. To stop the coach was impossible, but I was just able to check the pace sufficiently to enable me to pull across to the near side of the road, and pass on the wrong side.

In the case of a railway there would be no such chance. There they could only stop, or have an accident. One gets used to everything after a time, and, I suppose, if I had been an engine-driver, I should become so accustomed to this as to think nothing of it ; but, as it was, I never felt so helpless. I cannot conceive a greater trial of nerve than to be driving at the rate of twenty miles an hour, or more, among a labyrinth of rails, and entirely dependent on other people for safety.

It is not very long ago since I saw in a newspaper an account of a pointsman being found dead in his box !

I am reminded of the hackneyed saying of an old coachman in the early days of railways : " If a coach is upset," he said, " why, there you are ; but if an accident happens to a railway train, where are you ? "

It is now upwards of twenty years since the last time I handled four-horse reins, and more than fifty-five since the first time, and I am not going to say that no improvements have taken place during that

18

long period of time. Possibly some may have been
found, but I must confess that those I have heard of
do not appear to me to come into that category.

It is a common reply to those who stand up for old
systems that they were slow. That, at any rate,
can hardly be alleged in the present case, for, though
I admire the very smart thing done by poor Selby
between London and Brighton, I think, when we
consider the fast work habitually done in coaches in
days of yore, and still more on the first of May and
other special occasions, it must be admitted that the
pace has, to say the least, not increased. Indeed,
allowing for stoppages, taking up and putting down
passengers, which lost many minutes in a journey,
and the heavy loads carried, by neither of which
was the "Old Times" troubled, I think the
Brighton feat, good as it was, has often been
surpassed. The three Birmingham Tally-ho's generally had a spurt on the first of May, and more than
once performed the journey of a hundred and eight
miles under seven hours—the best record, I believe,
in existence.

Pace, however, at last, is a relative thing, and
eight or nine miles an hour on one road may be really
as fast as twelve or thirteen on another. I can safely
say that, though I have driven some fast coaches in
my time, I never had a day of harder work to keep
time than in doing eighty miles in ten hours. What

with one weak team in the early part of the journey, hilly roads, a heavy load, and frequent delays for changing passengers and luggage, the last stage of nine miles had to be covered in forty-two minutes to bring us in to time and catch the train.

Before finally bidding adieu to the subject of driving, it may perhaps be allowed me to say a few words about harness and the fitting of it. Of course it hardly needs saying that a coachman *ought* to be familiar with every strap and buckle of it, though this intimate knowledge may be dispensed with by those who only drive their own teams, and are always waited on by one or two good and experienced servants. Indeed, from what I witnessed in Hyde Park several years ago, I have had my suspicions whether these same servants are not sometimes utilised on early mornings in training the teams, and putting them straight for the masters' driving in the afternoon. I once saw a drag brought round to the right at the Magazine without the gentleman in charge of the box touching the off-side reins with his right hand at all ; and I fail to see how this could have been accomplished unless the horses were as well trained to it as circus steeds.

Still, however perfect these men may be as gentlemen's servants, their experience has not generally led them to attend very closely to the exact fitting of the harness—the collars particularly—which used often to be the plague of their lives to stage coachmen, and even might give trouble to a gentleman, if driving an extended tour. A few hints, therefore, from an old hand may perhaps not be thrown away. With horses freshly put into harness their shoulders are always liable to be rubbed, and they require the greatest care and attention; and one thing should always be insisted on in these cases, which is to wash the shoulders with cold water after work, and to leave the collars on till they have become quite dry again. But if care is necessary in the case of gentlemen's work, what must have been that required with coach horses—especially if running over long stages, with heavy loads and in hot weather. Of course, a good deal depended upon the care of the horse-keeper; but nothing he could do had any chance of keeping the shoulders sound if the collars "*wobbled*," which they certainly always will do if the least light can be seen between the collar and the upper part of the horse's neck. Then, again, it is most important for the collar to be the right length to suit the individual horse. One which carries his head high will require a longer one in proportion than one which carries it low, because the former position of the head has the effect of causing the windpipe to protrude. On stage-coach work we never cared so much about the weight of the collar as the fitting, and offering a fairly broad surface to the pressure. Two or three pounds extra weight in a collar is nothing

compared to the comfortable fitting of it, as we ourselves know to be the case with half-a-pound or so
when walking a long distance in strong boots.

If a wound should appear, after all the care that
can be taken, a paste made of fullers' earth with some
weak salt and water will nearly always effect a cure, if
the collar is properly chambered, so as to remove all
pressure from the part. In case of a shoulder showing a disposition to gall, I always carried in the hind
boot two or three small pads, which I could strap on
to the collar, so as to remove the pressure temporarily
till it could be chambered; and any gentleman embarking on a driving tour would find this to be a
good precaution to take, especially if he is going into
out-of-the-way districts.

I will conclude in the words of Horace—

> "Si quid noviste rectius istis,
> Candidus imperti : si non his utere mecum."

CHAPTER XXIV.

THE END OF THE JOURNEY.

AND now, ladies and gentlemen, "I leave you here," and trust I have given you no cause for complaint on the score of either civility or politeness to my passengers. I fear that in some places the road may have been heavy and the pace slow. Perhaps it may be thought that the style is incoherent, to which I can only say that such is usually the character of chatter; and if I have written anything which has afforded some interest or amusement, my most ardent hopes are satisfied.

The tale I have told has, in one sense, been told before, but so many fresh phases and incidents were so constantly turning up in the old mode of travelling, that it is not necessarily a twice-told tale. Probably the first idea of most readers upon closing the book will be, "How thankful I am that my lot was not cast in the days of my father or grandfather;" and this naturally leads to the reflection that when the busy wit of man had not produced so many inventions for evading the minor ills of life, the first idea was to endure them ; but now, when fresh schemes of all sorts and descriptions are being propounded every day to render life easy, it is to cure them ; and if this does not go to the length of making artificial wants, no doubt it is the wisest course to adopt.

To the old hand, however, who has not forgotten his early experiences, this eagerness to escape all hardship may seem to savour of softness and effeminacy, but I make no doubt that, though not called forth as it used to be in the days of yore, there still exists in the youth and manhood of Old England the same pluck and power of endurance when duty calls, as there ever was ; and that as long as we continue to cherish our old field sports and games, we are not in much danger of losing them.

It were folly to stand up for road travelling as against the greater convenience of railways ; still, I confess to a lingering feeling of regret that what was brought to such a state of perfection should have so completely vanished, and I think I cannot express these feelings better than by a short anecdote.

Many years ago, when hunting with the late Sir W. W. Wynn's hounds, when they had the advantage of the guidance of John Walker, I asked him which pack, whether the large or small, showed the best sport and killed the most foxes. His answer was, " Well, I really think the large pack does kill most foxes and give the best sport altogether, but *I like the little ones.*" And if asked which is the best mode of travelling, whether by road or rail, I must confess that, as a travelling machine for conveying us from one part of the country to another, the railway is the best both for safety, speed, and economy; but having said this, I am constrained to make the same sort of reservation as was made by John Walker, and say, "*I like the coaches.*"

Most noticeable of all, perhaps, was the plucky effort made in 1837 to revive the favourite "Red Rover" coach between London and Manchester, which had been discontinued upon the opening of the London and Birmingham and the Grand Junction Railways. It was "the last charge of the Old Guard," and shared the same fate. It may be interesting, however, to append a copy of this singular notice—one more evidence of the reluctance of Englishmen to be beaten, even at long odds. The very date at foot is significant, for the enterprise was embarked on in the teeth of the approaching winter.

THE RED ROVER REËSTABLISHED THROUGHOUT TO MANCHESTER.

Bull and Mouth Inn.

It is with much satisfaction that the Proprietors of the RED ROVER Coach are enabled to announce its

REËSTABLISHMENT

as a direct conveyance THROUGHOUT BETWEEN LONDON AND MANCHESTER, and that the arrangements will be the same as those which before obtained for it such entire and general approval.

In this effort the Proprietors anxiously hope that the public will recognize and appreciate the desire to supply an accommodation which will require and deserve the patronage and support of the large and busy community on that line of road.

The **RED ROVER** will start every evening, at a quarter before seven, by way of

COVENTRY	STAFFORD	MACCLESFIELD
BIRMINGHAM	NEWCASTLE-	AND
WALSALL	UNDER-LYNE	STOCKPORT
	CONGLETON	

and perform the journey *in the time which before gave such general satisfaction.*

☞ It will also start from the "Moseley Arms" Hotel, MANCHESTER, for LONDON, every evening, at nine o'clock.

EDWARD SHERMAN } *Joint*
JOHN WEATHERALD and Co. } *Proprietors.*

LONDON,
October 28, 1837.

An old song may come in here :—

> "The road, the road, the turnpike road,
>   The hard, the brown, the smooth, the broad,
>   Without a mark, without a bend,
>   Horses 'gainst horses on it contend.
>   Men laugh at the gates, they bilk the tolls,
>   Or stop and pay like honest souls.
>   I'm on the road, I'm on the road,
>   I'm never so blithe as when abroad
>   With the hills above and the vales below,
>   And merry wheresoe'er I go.
>   If the Opposition appear in sight,
>   What matter, what matter, we'll set that all right."

In the introduction I ventured to point out some inaccuracies which I had observed in a statement made upon the subject of coach fares, and as it is probably one which few remember anything about, I give a statement of what would be about the profit and loss of a month's working of a coach for a hundred miles.

RECEIPTS.				PAYMENTS.			
A Full Load on the Way-bill both ways.				Daily.	£	s.	d.
				15 toll-gates, at 3s.* . .	2	5	0
	£	s.	d.	Hire of coach, per mile 2½d.	1	0	10
8 inside passengers . .	15	0	0	Mileage duty, 2d.† . .	0	16	8
14 outside	25	4	0	Washing and oiling			
Parcels	1	0	0	coaches	0	2	0
	£41	4	0		£4	8	6

* It was usual for coaches to come to terms with the pikers to pay for three horses instead of four.

† There had also to be paid £5 licence duty yearly when the plates were taken out.

RECEIPTS (*continued*)—				PAYMENTS (*continued*)—			
	£	s.	d.		£	s.	d.
Month's receipts . . .	988	16	0	For 4 weeks	106	4	0
Deduct expenses . . .	113	14	0	*Monthly.*			
	£875	2	0	8 road booking-offices .	4	0	0
				2 end do.	2	0	0
				Making Share bills . .	1	0	0
				Oil and trimming lamps,			
				say	0	10	0
				Total £113	113	14	0

This makes £8 15s. to be divided per mile, which, of course, would give a very handsome profit; but full loading could not be expected every day, and if it was reduced to half loads, it would not be such a very fat concern.

The cost of each horse was usually put at 17s. 6d. a week, including blacksmith, and that, supposing a man to cover a ten-mile stage for which eight horses would be ample if not running on Sundays, would cost £7 a week, or £28 a month, leaving, at about half loading, say £20 profit. But from this has to be deducted saddler, veterinary surgeon, and wear and tear, the two latter of which depend, to a certain extent, on circumstances over which he has not much control, as it depends upon such things as sickness in the stables and accidents.

His Majesty's Mails.

V. R.

G. P. O.

APPENDIX.

LIST OF MAIL COACHES WHICH WORKED OUT OF LONDON.

Bath, through	Hounslow, Maidenhead, Reading, Newbury, Hungerford, Marlborough, Devizes,	From the "Spread Eagle," Gracechurch Street, and "Swan with Two Necks," Lad Lane.
Birmingham, through	Aylesbury, Bicester, Banbury, Leamington, Warwick,	From the "King's Arms," Holborn Bridge.
Brighton, through	Croydon, Reigate, Crawley, Cuckfield,	From the "Blossoms Inn," Lawrence Lane.
Bristol, through	Hounslow, Reading, Newbury, Marlborough, Calne, Chippenham, Bath,	From the "Swan with Two Necks," Lad Lane.

Carlisle—*See Glasgow.*

Chester, through	Barnet, St. Albans, Dunstable, Northampton, Hinckley, Atherstone, Lichfield, Stafford, Nantwich, Tarporley,	From the " Golden Cross," Charing Cross.
Devonport, through	Hounslow, Bagshot, Basingstoke, Andover, Salisbury, Sherborne, Chard, Honiton, Exeter	From the " Swan with Two Necks," Lad Lane.
Dover, through	Dartford, Rochester, Sittingbourne, Faversham, Canterbury,	From the " Swan with Two Necks," Lad Lane.
Edinburgh, through	Ware, Buntingford, Royston, Caxton, Huntingdon, Grantham Newark Doncaster	From the " Bull and Mouth," St. Martin's-le-Grand.

Edinburgh, through (*continued*).	Ferry Bridge, York, Northallerton, Darlington, Durham, Newcastle, Alnwick, Berwick, Dunbar, Haddington,	From the "Bull and Mouth," St. Martin's-le-Grand.
Exeter, through	Basingstoke, Andover, Salisbury, Blandford, Dorchester, Bridport, Axminster, Honiton,	From the "Bull and Mouth," St. Martin's-le-Grand.
Glasgow, through	Barnet, Hatfield, Baldock, Biggleswade, Stilton, Stamford, Grantham, Newark, Doncaster, Wetherby, Boroughbridge, Greta Bridge, Appleby, Carlisle,	From the "Bull and Mouth," St. Martin's-le-Grand.

Gloucester, through	Hounslow, Maidenhead, Henley, Nettlebed, Oxford Witney, Burford, Cheltenham,	From the "Cross Keys," Wood Street, and "Golden Cross," Charing Cross.
Halifax, through	Barnet, Woburn, Newport-Pagnel, Market Harborough, Nottingham, Sheffield, Huddersfield,	From the "Swan with Two Necks," Lad Lane, and "Bull and Mouth," St. Martin's-le-Grand.
Hastings, through	Farnborough, Tunbridge, Lamberhurst,	From the "Golden Cross," Charing Cross, and "Bolt in Tun," Fleet Street.
Holyhead, through	Barnet, St. Albans, Coventry, Birmingham, Wolverhampton, Shrewsbury, Oswestry, North Wales,	From the "Swan with Two Necks," Lad Lane.

Manchester, through	Barnet, St. Albans, Dunstable, Northampton, Market Harborough, Leicester, Derby, Ashbourne, Congleton, Macclesfield,	From the "Swan with Two Necks," Lad Lane.
Norwich, by Ipswich, through	Ilford, Romford, Brentwood, Chelmsford, Witham, Colchester,	From the "Spread Eagle," Gracechurch Street.
Norwich, by Newmarket, through	Epping, Bury St. Edmunds, Thetford,	From the "Belle Sauvage," Ludgate Hill.
Portsmouth, through	Kingston, Esher, Guildford, Godalming, Petersfield,	From the "White Horse," Fetter Lane, and "Bolt in Tun," Fleet Street.
Southampton and Poole, through	Hounslow, Staines, Bagshot, Alton, Alresford, Winchester,	From the "Swan with Two Necks," Lad Lane, and "Bell and Crown," Holborn.

Stroud, through	Hounslow, Henley, Abingdon, Faringdon, Cirencester,	From the "Cross Keys," Wood Street, and the "Swan with Two Necks," Lad Lane.
Wells (Norfolk), through	Lynn, Ely, Cambridge, Royston, Ware,	From the "Swan with Two Necks," Lad Lane.
Worcester, through	Uxbridge, Beaconsfield, High Wycombe, Oxford, Woodstock, Chipping Norton, Moreton-in-Marsh, Evesham, Pershore,	From the "Bull and Mouth," St. Martin's-le-Grand.
Yarmouth, through	Romford, Chelmsford, Witham, Colchester, Ipswich, Saxmundham, Lowestoft,	From the "White Horse," Fetter Lane.

So much for the main arteries, but the account would hardly be complete without showing how the more remote and out-of-the-way districts were provided for. I will, therefore, add the routes of a few mails which might be considered as prolongations of some of those already mentioned, but they were worked under fresh contracts and with fresh coaches.

South Wales was served by three—one from Bristol and two from Gloucester, as shown below :—

Bristol to
Milford Haven,
by
{
New Passage Ferry,
Newport,
Cardiff,
Cowbridge,
Neath,
Caermarthen.
}

Gloucester to
Milford Haven,
by
{
Ross,
Monmouth,
Abergavenny,
Brecon,
Llandovery,
Caermarthen,
Haverfordwest.
}

Gloucester to Aberystwith, by
Ross, Hereford, Kington, Rhayader, and Dyffryn Castle.

The Gloucester and Milford was, I think, driven out of Gloucester at one time by Jack Andrews, a very good coachman, and over the lower ground there was a man of the name of Jones. I may, perhaps, be told that that is not a very distinguishing mark of a man in those parts, perhaps it is not, but if the name failed to convey a knowledge of who he was, he, at any rate, possessed one very characteristic feature which was that he always drove without gloves whatever might be the state of the weather. If he saw his box passenger beating his hands against his body or going through any other process with the vain hope of restoring the circulation into his well-nigh frozen fingers, his delight was to hold out his gloveless hand and say, " Indeed, now there is a hand that never wore a glove."

And this recalls to my memory another anecdote which was told me a great many years ago, and which, though it refers to the other extremities, may not be inappropriately introduced here. It appertains to a very well known character already mentioned, the well known Billy Williams, often spoken of as Chester Billy. I am aware that tales are sometimes engrafted on remarkable characters which are also told of others, still I believe I shall not be doing a wrong to any one if I tell this as "'twas told to me," of our old friend Billy. At any rate, it is too good to be lost, so here it is.

On one very cold winter morning it happened that Billy had a box passenger who was stamping his feet on the foot-board in the vain attempt to restore the circulation of the blood, which led Billy to remark, "Your feet seem cold this morning, sir," to which the gentleman answered, " I should think they were, are not yours ? " " No," says Billy, "they're not ; " adding, " I expect you wash 'em." "Wash them," says the passenger, "of course I do, don't you ? " " No," was the reply, " I should think not, I *iles* 'em."

The Manchester mail was also prolonged to Carlisle, though the direct Carlisle mail went by a rather shorter route, but then the populous district on the west coast had to be provided for. It travelled through Preston, Lancaster, Kendal and Penrith. This was, over some of the ground at any rate, one of the fastest mails in England.

Again, in addition to these, which may be said to have had their origin in London, there existed a considerable number of what were called " cross country mails," some of which ran long distances and at high speed, connecting together many important districts. A few of them I will mention, beginning with the Bristol and Liverpool, which was a very fast one.

Bristol to Liverpool, by	Aust Passage Ferry, Monmouth, Hereford, Shrewsbury, Chester, Woodside Ferry.
Bristol to Oxford, by	Bath, Tetbury, Cirencester, Fairford, Faringdon.
Liverpool to Hull, by	Warrington, Manchester, Rochdale, Halifax, Bradford, Leeds, Tadcaster, York.
Bristol to Birmingham, by	Gloucester, Wincanton, Droitwich, Bromsgrove.
Birmingham to Sheffield, by	Lichfield, Derby, Chesterfield.

And no doubt there were several others in one part of

the country or another, but I have been unable to meet with any regular list of them, though it is very unlikely that such a road as that between Bristol and Exeter by Taunton, for example, should have been left out. This road certainly had a fast coach on it. The " Royal Exeter " ran from Cheltenham to Exeter through Gloucester and Bristol, driven between Cheltenham and Bristol at one time by Capt. Probyn, and afterwards by William Small. It was a fast coach, stopping for dinner at Nisblete's, at Bristol, and then proceeding on its journey to Exeter.

Then, again, there was a populous and important district through the Staffordshire Potteries, from Birmingham to Liverpool and Manchester, which must have been provided for somehow, but it is not impossible that this may have been effected by the bags being conveyed to Lichfield by the Sheffield, and then transferred to the down Liverpool and Chester mails.

There were also running short distances what were called third class mails, which carried twelve passengers, and the coachman was in charge of the bags. On one of them which ran between Shrewsbury and Newtown I did a good deal of my early practice.

And now, having given a list, more or less perfect, of the mails which traversed England and Wales, perhaps a few words on the subject of the pace at which they travelled may not be without interest.

After singling out the London and Birmingham day mail, which was timed at twelve miles an hour, it is impossible to say, at the present date, which was the fastest coach. That the " Quicksilver " was the fastest mail, I have no doubt, though I believe the palm has been disputed by the Bristol, and perhaps some others ; for if a passenger asked a coachman which was the fastest, he was very likely to be told that the one he was travelling in was. I cannot, however, believe that any of these claims could have been supported by facts.

" *Cui bono ?* "   We can see at a glance why the Devonport
should be pushed along as fast as possible, because the
journey was a long one ; but the distance to Bristol was only
one hundred and twenty miles, and whether the mail arrived
there at eight or nine o'clock in the morning would have been
thought little of in those days, but in a journey of two
hundred and twenty-seven miles half a mile an hour makes
an appreciable difference.   It would seem reasonable, therefore, that the longer mails should have been accelerated as
much as possible, and so I believe it really was the case, and
that the Holyhead was, after the " Quicksilver," the fastest
out of London.   At any rate, I know that, when travelling
by it, we always passed all the other mails going the same
road, and that included a considerable number, as the north
road and the Holyhead were synonymous as far as Barnet,
and, moreover, the post office was likely to have screwed up
these two mails the tightest, as one carried the Irish bags and
the other had the correspondence of an important dockyard
and naval station.

To single out the fastest coach would be still more impossible.   The "Wonder" had a world-wide reputation,
which was well deserved, both for the pace and regularity
with which she travelled and the admirable manner in which
she was appointed in every way ; but what gave that coach
its preponderating name was the fact of its being the first
which undertook to be a day coach over a distance much
exceeding one hundred and twenty miles.   The Manchester
Telegraph must have surpassed the "Wonder" in pace, and,
certainly, when we consider the difference of the roads and
the hills by which she was opposed in her journey through
Derbyshire, had the most difficult task to accomplish ; and,
again, the "Hirondelle" was timed to go the journey of one
hundred and thirty-three miles between Cheltenham and
Liverpool in twelve hours and a half, which is a higher rate
of speed than the "Wonder," which was allowed fifteen and

a half hours to cover the one hundred and fifty-four miles between London and Shrewsbury, and on a far superior road.

I have been induced to enter into this subject because one sometimes now-a-days meets with people who appear to have a somewhat hazy idea about it, and talk glibly of twelve miles an hour as if it was nothing so very great after all. Well, I am not going to deny that it can be done, because I know that it has been effected by the Birmingham day mail, as already stated, and I have also been told by an old inspector of mails that in the latter days they did contrive to screw some Scotch mails up to that speed ; but I am sure I can safely say that no mail or stage-coach ever was timed at even eleven miles an hour during the main coaching days, however much faster they might have gone when racing or on special occasions, though I believe it would have been attempted, at any rate, if road travelling had not been put an end to by the railways.

Twelve miles an hour is very great work to accomplish. Why, when stoppages of all sorts are allowed for, it means thirteen miles, and that means galloping for the greater part of the way.

THOUGH the subjoined List is not comprehensive, nor indeed absolutely accurate, it may be worth inserting, as conveying a fair idea of what coaches ran.

	PRINCIPAL NIGHT MAILS		Time (including stoppages) of Mail.		SOME NOTED DAY COACHES.
Miles from London.	TO		h.	m.	
110½	BATH		11	0	"Beaufort Hunt," "York House," "White Hart," "Times."
50	BEDFORD		.	.	
119	BIRMINGHAM		11	56	{ "Tally-Ho," "Tantivy," "Greyhound," "Economist," "Rocket," "Eclipse," "Triumph," "Crown Prince," "Emerald," "Albion," "Day," etc.
	BRECON		.	.	"Red Rover."
53	BRIGHTON		.	.	{ "Red Rover," "Times," "Age," "Quicksilver," "Pearl," "Dart," "Arrow," "Vivid."
121	BRISTOL		11	45	"Prince of Wales," "Monarch," "Regulator."
50	CAMBRIDGE		.	.	"Star."
95	CHELTENHAM (see below)		.	.	"Berkeley Hunt," "Rival," "Magnet," "Favourite."
181	CHESTER		.	.	"Criterion."
217½	DEVONPORT		23	45	"Quicksilver."
71	DOVER		19	0	{ "Telegraph" (165 miles) 17 hours; "Defiance" (168 miles), 19 hours; "Nonpareil," "Herald."
176	EXETER		.	.	
111	GLOUCESTER		11	55	"Hope."
195½	HALIFAX		20	5	
68	HASTINGS		.	.	"Champion," "Tiger."
135	HEREFORD		26	55	
259	HOLYHEAD		18	12	
172½	HULL		21	0	"Courier," "Rockingham."
197	LEEDS		20	50	"Umpire," "Fair Trader," "Express," "Erin-go-bragh."
201½	LIVERPOOL				

Miles	Destination	H.	M.	Coaches
148	LOUTH	16	0	
99	LYNN	10	33	
185	MANCHESTER	19	0	"Telegraph" (186 miles), 18 hours 15 minutes, "Beehive," "Estafette," "Peveril of the Peak," "Cobourg," "Red Rover."
129	MONMOUTH	.	.	"Mazeppa," "Royal Forester."
113½	NORWICH *via* IPSWICH	11	38	"Shannon."
117½	„ *via* NEWMARKET	13	0	"Phenomenon."
106	POOLE	.	.	"Phœnix."
73	PORTSMOUTH	.	.	"Diligence," "Regulator," "Hero."
158	SHREWSBURY	.	.	"Wonder," 15 hours 45 minutes; "Nimrod," "Stag," "Union," "Oxonian."
	SOUTHAMPTON	.	.	"Star."
105	STROUD	12	9	"King's Royal."
195	WETHERBY (Glasgow Mail)	20	36	"Taglioni."
128	WEYMOUTH	.	.	
23	WINDSOR	.	.	"Wellington."
114	WORCESTER	12	20	
197	YORK (Edinburgh Mail)	20	54	
30	LIVERPOOL AND PRESTON	.	.	"Defiance" (12 hrs. 10 min., including 30 min. Ferry).
129¼	EDINBURGH AND ABERDEEN	.	.	"Hirondelle," "Hibernia" (*see above*).
	CHELTENHAM AND LIVERPOOL	.	.	"Royal Oak," "Nettle," "Engineer."
	SHREWSBURY AND WELSHPOOL AND ABERYSTWITH	.	.	

NOTES.

The fastest coaches were the "Defiance" (Edinburgh and Aberdeen), the "Wonder" (Shrewsbury and London), for which alone 150 horses were kept, and the mail from Liverpool to Preston. The next fastest were the Holyhead, Exeter, and Scotch mails, and those to Bath and Bristol (which last ones did not stop for meals on the road). The slowest is the Stroud mail, but formerly was the Worcester mail, which used to be most frequently overturned of any. The Hastings and Brighton mails had only two horses. For some reason or other, with which I am not acquainted, the Liverpool mail, and, I believe, the Halifax also, though leaving London at the same time as the others, had a day coach on the up journey, arriving at St. Martin's-le-Grand about 7 p.m. One of the Birmingham coaches was lighted by gas for a time, as far back as 1834. A coach running *every* day between London and Birmingham paid annually for toll-gates the sum of £1,428. The double miles of the mails travelling reached at one time 6,619 a journey.

SCOTCH AND IRISH MAILS.

IT is interesting to compare the running of the Edinburgh
and Glasgow coaches out of London. Both left St. Martin's
at the same hour, but by a different road. At Alconbury (65
miles out of London) the two coaches must have frequently
been in sight of each other on a moonlight night—if punctual
a bare four minutes divided them (not a yokel in that part of
Huntingdonshire but could discuss the merits of the rival
whips)—and at Grantham (108 miles out) they probably
transferred some mail bags picked up upon their different
roads.

At Doncaster (159 miles from London) less than a
quarter of an hour divided the two vehicles after travelling
all through the night and portion of the following day, a feat
successfully performed that would make the hair of a modern
South-Eastern Railway guard stand upon end. Indeed,
tradition says that the up and down coaches nearly always
" crossed " within a few yards of the same bridge. Even that
northern metropolis, Newcastle, was treated with scant
ceremony ; as soon as fresh horses were attached and the
mail bags exchanged, the coach went forward without pause,
the next " stop and examine coach " after York being at
Belford (near Berwick-upon-Tweed).

With the Edinburgh coach there were three halts only
upon the road for refreshments, and these were liable to
curtailment in heavy weather when any minutes had been
lost on the way—at the ordinary stages the changes of horses
being sometimes made in less than a minute.

The Glasgow coach, though over a considerably more uneven road, was slightly the quicker of the two, the rival distances by road being almost identical. This coach was not encumbered with heavy bags for the Highlands, and had the additional stimulus for the first dozen miles or so out of London of racing the Holyhead mail through Barnet. This celebrated mail made its " first stop " (other than for change of horses) at Birmingham, its second at Shrewsbury, its third at Corwen, and its fourth at Bangor. The speed of this mail was no less than nine and three-quarters miles an hour, or over ten miles if stoppages are taken into account.

At Shrewsbury five minutes only were allowed for refreshments, and the timing of this coach was so close that it was due there one minute before the beautiful, varied, and sonorous clocks of that proud borough struck the hour of noon (11.59 a.m.). At Wolverhampton it was timed to arrive also at one minute past the hour (9.1 a.m), while the timepieces of the guards were checked once or twice on the road by special clocks, and the discrepancy, if any, taken note of in writing.

Another notable piece of "good running" was shown by the rival mails to Caermarthen, which reached there from town the following evening. The Gloucester coach arrived at eight o'clock (224 miles), and was followed at only half-an-hour's interval by the Bristol (238 miles) coming by a different road the whole journey, and having often to face a rough sea when transferring its passengers at Aust Passage, near Chepstow. This last mail was one of the quickest of all out of London ; as far as Bristol it was expedited in 1837 to run at the speed of ten miles and three furlongs an hour, prior to which time it had to cede the palm to the celebrated Falmouth (or, as it was often miscalled, Devonport—confusing it with the Plymouth coach) Quicksilver mail. No doubt a higher speed still would have been attained in the winter months had these coaches not to include so much night work in their running.

It is very difficult, unless precise dates are attached, to give now the absolute distances travelled. Each year roads were straightened out and bends removed, gradients modified, or minor deviations to towns of less importance struck out. A list of such accelerations will be found in Mogg's edition of Paterson and of the principal ordinary routes traversed in Paterson, Leigh, or Cary.

What prospects the Coventry bicycle might have had *before* the arrival of the telegraph and railway epoch it is difficult to conjecture; but its speed must then have placed it in the first rank of means of locomotion.

1837. Scotch Mails. DOWN.

TO THURSO VIÂ EDINBURGH.

Miles.	*St. Martin's-le-Grand.*			
	LONDON	dep.	p.m. 8. 0	night
12½	Waltham Cross	arr.	9.25	—
22	Ware	,,	10.26	—
35¼	Buckland	,,	11.52	—
45½	Arrington	,,	a.m. 12.57	—
60	HUNTINGDON	,,	2.30	—
65¼	Alconbury Hill	,,	3. 3	—
72¼	Stilton	,,	3.45	—
87	STAMFORD	,,	5.15	—
95	Stretton	,,	6. 3	day
108½	GRANTHAM	arr.	7.23	—
		dep.	8. 3	—
115¾	Long Bennington.	arr.	8.53	—
122¼	NEWARK	,,	9.30	—
132¾	Scarthing Moor	,,	10.34	—
145½	Barnby Moor	,,	11.49	—
155¼	Rossington Bridge	,,	p.m. 12.47	—
159½	DONCASTER	,,	1.12	—
166¼	Askerne	,,	1.55	—
179¾	Selby	,,	3.21	—
194	YORK	arr.	4.54	—
		dep.	5.34	—
207¼	Easingwold	arr.	6.54	night
218	Thirsk	,,	7.58	—
227	NORTHALLERTON	,,	8.52	—
243	DARLINGTON	,,	10.28	—
261½	DURHAM	,,	a.m. 12.23	—
276	NEWCASTLE-ON-TYNE	arr.	1.50	—
		dep.	1.53	—
290½	Morpeth	arr.	3.22	—
300½	Felton	,,	4.23	—
309¾	ALNWICK	,,	5.17	—
324½	BELFORD	arr.	6.47	day
		dep.	7.17	—
339¾	BERWICK-ON-TWEED	arr.	8.47	—
353½	Houndswood	,,	10. 9	—
369¼	Dunbar	,,	11.41	—
380¼	Haddington	,,	p.m. 12.45	—
397¼	EDINBURGH G.P.O.	,,	2.23	—

(*Time on road* 42 h. 23 m. *The quickest train time the journey has been performed in was on August* 31, 1888, *when the King's Cross train arrived in* 7 h. 27 m.)

444	Perth	arr.	9. 0	night
466	Dundee	,,	11.15	—
534	Aberdeen	,,	a.m. 6.22	day
641	Inverness	,,	p.m. 8. 6	night
783	Thurso	,,	a.m. 8.10	day

TO GLASGOW.

Miles.	*St. Martin's-le-Grand.*			
	LONDON	dep.	p.m. 8. 0	night
11¼	Barnet	arr.	9.18	—
25¼	Welwyn	,,	10.46	—
37½	Baldock	,,	a.m. 12. 6	—
46¾	Caldecot	,,	1. 2	—
55¼	Eaton	,,	1.55	—
65¾	Alconbury Church	,,	2.59	—
75¼	Stilton	,,	3.56	—
90	STAMFORD	,,	5.28	—
98	Stretton	,,	6.18	day
111½	GRANTHAM	arr.	7.40	—
		dep.	8.20	—
117½	Foston	arr.	8.56	—
125½	NEWARK	,,	9.44	—
138½	Ollerton	,,	11. 3	—
143	Worksop	,,	11.52	—
151½	Bagley	,,	p.m. 12.40	—
159¾	DONCASTER	,,	1.26	—
174¼	Pontefract	,,	2.53	—
	*** *Change for* LEEDS *and* WAKEFIELD.			
184¼	Aberford	arr.	3.52	—
	*** *Change for* BRADFORD.			
191¾	WETHERBY	arr.	4.36	—
		dep.	5.11	—
	*** *Change here for* YORK.			
204	Boroughbridge	arr.	6.23	night
216	Leeming	,,	7.35	—
227	Catterick Bridge	,,	8.41	—
236	Foxhall	,,	9.35	—
240½	Greta Bridge	,,	10. 2	—
250½	New Spital	,,	11.10	—
260	Brough	,,	a.m. 12.15	—
268	APPLEBY	,,	1. 7	—
282	PENRITH	,,	2.28	—
293	Hesketh	,,	3.23	—
	Manchester Mail 3.0 p.m., *reaches Carlisle G.P.O.* 4.48 a.m.			
303	CARLISLE G.P.O.	arr.	4.17	—
		dep.	5. 0	—
312¾	Gretna	arr.	5.55	—
322	Ecclefechan	,,	6.48	day
332¾	Dunwoodie	,,	7.49	—
342½	Beattock Bridge	,,	8.42	—
361	Abington	,,	10.26	—
370	Douglas Mill	,,	11.18	—
376	Lesmahagow Bar.	,,	bags dropped.	
387¼	Hamilton	,,	p.m. 12.57	—
397¾	GLASGOW G.P.O.	,,	2. 0	—

(*Time on road*, 42 *hours.*)

TO KINGSTOWN VIÂ HOLYHEAD.

Miles.	*St. Martin's-le-Grand.*		n.m.	
	LONDON .... dep.		8. o	night
11¼	Barnet .... arr.		—	—
20½	St. Albans..........	,,	—	—
24½	Redbourne	,,	10.44	—
33½	DUNSTABLE	,,	—	—
			a.m.	
42¼	Brickhill.............	,,	12.32	—
51¼	Stony Stratford...	,,	1.26	—
59	Towcester	,,	2.12	—
71¼	Daventry	,,	3.25	—
79	Dunchurch.........	,,	4.11	—
90¼	COVENTRY.........	,,	5.18	—
108½	BIRMINGHAM { arr.		7. 8	day
	{ dep.		7.43	—
116½	Wednesbury .... arr.		8.28	—
122	WOLVERHAMPTON	,,	9. 1	—
134½	Shiffnal	,,	10.14	—
142¼	Heygate Junction.	,,	10.59	—
144½	Wellington	,,	11.20	—
152½	SHREWSBURY { arr.		11.59	—
	{ dep.		p.m. 12. 4	—
161	Netcliffe .... arr.		12.52	—
170½	OSWESTRY..........	,,	1.45	—
176¼	Chirk.............	,,	—	—
183	LLANGOLLEN	,,	2.57	—
193¼	CORWEN....... { arr.		3.57	—
	{ dep.		4.25	—
199½	Tynant............. arr.		5. 1	—
206¼	Cernioge............	,,	5.39	—
213½	"New Stables"..	,,	6.21	night
220¾	Capel Curig	,,	7. 2	—
228¼	Tyn-y-maes	,,	7.46	—
	BANGOR......... { arr.		8.20	—
	{ dep.		8.25	—
	Anglesea Ferry.... arr.		8.43	—

Here cross the Menai Straits at night by ferry until the opening of Telford's Suspension Bridge, in 1826.

	Mona Inn........... arr.		9.43	—
259	Holyhead Post { arr.		10.55	—
	Office............ { dep.			
323	Kingstown .... arr.			
327	Dublin...............	,,		

(*Time on journey,* h.   m.   *Present time on journey,* h.   m.)

TO WATERFORD (?) VIÂ GLOUCESTER AND MILFORD.

Miles.	*St. Martin's-le-Grand.*		n.m.	
	LONDON .. .. dep.		8. o	night
12¼	Hounslow ...... arr.		9.20	—
19¾	Colnbrook	,,	—	—
23¾	Slough	,,	—	—
29	Maidenhead	,,	11. 8	—
38¼	Henley-on-Thames	,,	—	—
43	Nettlebed	,,	—	—
			a.m.	
61¼	OXFORD ...... { arr.		2.38	—
	{ dep.		—	—
72¾	Witney .... arr.		3.58	—
80	Burford	,,	—	—
89¾	Northleach.........	,,	5.43	—
97¼	Andoverford	,,	—	day
102¾	CHELTEN- { arr.		7. 3	—
	HAM .... { dep.		—	—
112	GLOUCES- { arr.		8. o	—
	TER .... { dep.		—	—
129	Ross .... arr.		10. 8	—
139	MONMOUTH	,,	11.11	—
			p.m.	
156	Abergavenny	,,	12.53	—
176	BRECON	,,	3. 1	—
197	Llandovery	,,	5.22	—
224	CARMARTHEN ...	,,	8. o	night
	Haverfordwest	,,		
	HUBBERSTON	,,		

..* Compare the quicker relative time to Carmarthen made by the Bristol mail immediately following, notwithstanding having to cross the Bristol Channel.*

TO WATERFORD (?) VIÂ BRISTOL AND PEMBROKE.

Miles.	*St. Martin's-le-Grand.*		p.m.	
	LONDON .... dep.		8. o	night
12¼	Hounslow .... arr.		9.12	—
29	Maidenhead	,,	10.50	—
	READING...........	,,	—	—
			a.m.	
59	Newbury....	,,	1.41	—
	Marlborough	,,	—	—
90	CALNE.............	,,	4.49	—
	Chippenham.......	,,	—	—
109	BATH...............	,,	6.32	day
122	BRISTOL ...... { arr.		7.45	—
	{ dep.		—	—
134	New Passage Ferry arr.		9.12	—
	NEWPORT	,,	—	—
			p.m.	
166	CARDIFF	,,	12.53	—
	Cowbridge	,,	—	—
	Neath	,,	—	—
211	Swansea	,,	5.18	—
238	CARMARTHEN ...	,,	8.31	night
			a.m.	
273	Hobbs Point	,,	12.34	—
	Pembroke	,,	1. 9	—

Western and Foreign Mails. — 1837. — Up and Down.

Down

Miles	Station	Falmouth Mail†	Exeter Mail	Devonport Mail
	ST. MARTIN'S-LE-GRAND ...dep.	8. 0 p.m.	8. 0 p.m.	8. 0 p.m.
12	Hounslow ...arr.			
19	Staines		9.56	9.12
23	Slough			
29	Maidenhead			
58	Newbury			
77	Marlborough			
91	Devizes			
109	Bath			
149	Bridgewater			
160	TAUNTON			
180	Collumpton			
29	Bagshot	10.47 p.m.		10.40
67	Andover	2.20 a.m.	2.42 a.m.	1.53 a.m.
84	SALISBURY		4.27	3.43
126	Yeovil			5.6
143	Chard			7.0
80	Amesbury	3.39		11.30
125	Ilchester	7.50	11. 0	12.35 p.m.
	Honiton {arr. / dep.}	11. 0	12.31 p.m.	2.42
	EXETER {arr. / dep.}	12.34 p.m. / 12.44	2.12	
210	Newton			3.57
218	Totnes	2.41		
190	Ashburton	5.5		6.33
214	PLYMOUTH {arr. / dep.}	5.14		7.25
	DEVONPORT {arr. / dep.}			
234	Liskeard	7.55		10.5
246	Lostwithiel	9.12		
254	St. Austell	10.20		
268	TRURO	11.55		
279	FALMOUTH ...arr.	1. 5 a.m.		

Miles from London:—HONITON, via Amesbury, 151; via Salisbury, 156. EXETER, via Amesbury, 170; via Salisbury, 173; via Taunton, 193. DEVONPORT, via Amesbury, 216; via Taunton, 245.

† Note. The Falmouth mail was allowed 25 minutes stoppage at Ilminster (8.58 a.m. to 9.23), notwithstanding which it travelled between London and Exeter at the average speed of 10 miles and 2 furlongs an hour.

Up

Station	Falmouth Mail	Exeter Mail	Devonport Mail
Packet arrives from abroad.			
FALMOUTH ...dep.	1.45 a.m.		
TRURO ...arr.	2.55		
St. Austell	4.29		
Lostwithiel	5.36		
Liskeard	6.52		
DEVONPORT {rep. / dep.}			4.45 a.m.
PLYMOUTH	9.30		
Ashburton			
Totnes	12. 3 p.m.		7.30
Newton			8.25
EXETER {arr. / dep.}	2. 0 / 2.20	11.50 p.m. / 1.27 a.m.	10.15
Honiton			
Ilchester	4. 4	2.55	
Amesbury	6.49	4.30	
Chard		8.50	
Yeovil			
SALISBURY	11. 0	11. 0	
Andover			
Bagshot	12.19 a.m.		11.38
Collumpton			1.37 p.m
TAUNTON	4. 2		2.52
Bridgewater			7.30
BATH			9.24
Devizes			10.49
Marlborough			12.42 a.m.
Newbury			3.44
Maidenhead			
Slough			
Staines		3.46 p.m.	5 26
Hounslow			
ST. MARTIN'S-LE-GRAND ...arr.	6.50	5.42	6.40

Notes.—Greenwich time throughout. The mails left London one hour earlier (at 7.0 p.m.) on Sundays. The Falmouth (nicknamed the "Quicksilver") mail averaged over 10 miles an hour between London and Devonport.

Naval Station for the departure of the foreign packets.

SIMMONS & BOTTEN,
Printers,
LONDON, E.C.

Printed in the United States
107546LV00003B/116/A

9 780548 660195